Dréa's Dream:
An Unfinished Dance

Lessons of love, loss, hope, and healing

For
Linda & Kate

Passe On —
Dream always.

Sue Rizzo Visicaro

Dréa's Dream: An Unfinished Dance
Lessons of Love, Loss, Hope, and Healing

This book may be ordered online at:
www.SusanRizzoVincent.com
www.amazon.com

To protect their privacy, the author has changed the names
of some of the people who are in this book. Sequence of several events and
dates have been combined and condensed for readability.

ISBN –13: 978-1479389872
ISBN–10: 1479389870

Prose and poetry by Andréa Rizzo
Edited by Molly McKitterick
Copy edited by Lindsey Ulkus and Marcia Harriman
Cover Design and Photography by Theresa Smerud, Artist & Photographer
www.theresasmerud.com
Markham Starr, Fowler Road Press, No. Stonington, CT

If you would like Susan Rizzo Vincent to speak to your group or have a book
signing, contact her at SRizzoVincent@gmail.com

For information on
The Andréa Rizzo Foundation visit www.DreasDream.org

Dréa's Dream:
An Unfinished Dance

Lessons of love, loss, hope, and healing

Susan Rizzo Vincent
with
Andréa Rizzo

Foreword by
Jane Seymour

Dedication

This book is dedicated to my only child, Andréa. It was her idea to write a book that would inspire others who may be traveling the same path that we danced together. Woven throughout are poetic reflections that Andréa created as a young adult about her early childhood challenges. There were so many lessons we learned.

Andréa, I am so proud to continue the dance we began the day you were born.

We dance on.

Acknowledgments

Dréa's Dream: An Unfinished Dance would not be possible without the unconditional love and support of so many people who touched Andréa's life, and subsequently my life, and who are responsible for keeping her dream alive. I'm compelled to thank each and every one of them and have attempted to do that by having two sections of acknowledgements – both here and at the end of the book.

By opening myself up to their love, miracles occurred that ultimately have impacted thousands of children with cancer and special needs. For these gifts, I extend my sincerest thanks to the following:

My family for being there for me on this journey: My parents, Gloria and Vincent Bitetto; Andréa's aunts and uncles, Gary and Marilou Bitetto, Jill and Don Mollitor; Andréa's cousins, Jami Longo, Erika Bitetto, Gary Bitetto, Jr., Tayler Mollitor, Justin Bitetto and Makenzi Mollitor.

Those who unselfishly gave me encouragement when I needed it the most: Actress and artist, Jane Seymour for believing in my vision and giving me the precious gift of a beautifully written foreword; Susan Nagy Luks for telling me to never give up and patiently guiding me to be sure that I didn't; Mary Ann Marino for convincing me that this book must be written and for giving of her time so that it would be completed; Theresa Smerud for generously offering her artistic talent and never-ending patience; Markham Starr for his expert layout of this book; Sally Knowles for design help; Joan Alix for being there with encouraging words every step of the way; Barbara and Bob Ulkus and Karen and Mike Starkowski for being "my teams;" my editor, Molly McKitterick for her wisdom, and my copy editors, Lindsey Ulkus and Marcia Harriman for their attention to every detail. Special thanks to the following individuals who listened and advised over many phone calls, emails, dinners, and beach days: Rosanne Donner and Michael Pugh, Barbara Thompson, Lynn Audet, Jill Mollitor, Charles Margolis, Lisa DePrete, Laura Harlan, Martha Lynch and Aldo Passarelli, Terry Schimmel and my fellow writers in Lisa Tener's *Bring Your Book to Life* seminar.

Contents

Foreword

I first met Susan Rizzo Vincent when she was escorting a teenage cancer patient from New York City to *Dancing With the Stars* in Hollywood during the season when I performed on that show. I was immediately struck by her determination to help children through her non-profit organization.

Susan invited my support to help defray the cost of the patient's airfare, and I donated one of my first *Open Heart* paintings as an auction item to cover the child's travel costs.

As I learned more about the Andréa Rizzo Foundation and its pediatric dance therapy program, *Dréa's Dream*, created by Susan in memory of her daughter, I was moved by how she turned what might have been a crippling tragedy into a gift for children in need. She found a way to fulfill her daughter Andréa's dream of helping children with cancer and special needs to experience the benefits of dance/movement therapy. Susan garnered the support of young dancers across the nation who were inspired to make a difference by combining their own love of dance with compassion for children less fortunate than themselves.

Having been a dancer all of my life, I understood the impact that dance would have on a child's emotional and physical healing. When I spoke with administrators at Memorial Sloan-Kettering Cancer Center, Children's Hospital Los Angeles, and Mattel Children's Hospital UCLA, I heard testimony that convinced me that *Dréa's Dream* was not only helping their most fragile patients move and experience the joy of dance, but it also helped them to find new ways of expressing their emotions to better cope with their illness and even manage their pain.

Dréa's Dream: An Unfinished Dance will empower parents facing the devastating news of their child's cancer diagnosis and it will also empower parents of any child facing disabilities. In addition, it offers inspiration to dancers, who know firsthand the therapeutic value of dance as a healing modality, to nonprofit leaders, and to anyone who is looking for an inspiring story of a mother's and daughter's everlasting bond. For parents who have actually lost a child, this book provides a guiding light and offers help to find a reason to go on when such tragedy strikes.

Over the last several years, I have been impressed with Susan's dedication as she spreads *Dréa's Dream* to pediatric hospitals throughout the country. I have watched her tenaciously overcome adversity and create something positive and transformational for those in need, turning her own pain into a gift for others. When I decided to start The Open Hearts Foundation and honor those who epitomize the Open Heart philosophy of turning their own challenges into a way of helping others, I thought of Susan and her daughter Andréa. On February 19, 2011, Susan Rizzo

Vincent was one of the first four recipients of the Open Hearts Foundation Award along with Emmit and Pat Smith, Robin Roberts, and Jesse Billauer. I am proud to have supported the Andréa Rizzo Foundation as I believe in the power of dance and applaud the difference Susan Rizzo Vincent has made by opening her heart for thousands of children to benefit.

Dréa's Dream: An Unfinished Dance gives us an intimate look at how one parent continued to look deep within to find what is possible when faced with the seemingly impossible and in so doing, has made a difference that will impact children well into the future. Enjoy this uplifting story of triumph.

Jane Seymour
~ Actress, Artist, and Philanthropist

Prologue

February 19, 2011

It's a perfect morning for strolling down the boardwalk from Santa Monica to Venice Beach. The sun is on the rise and the temperature is delightful. It's not too hot, and I'm glad I grabbed my favorite blue cotton sweater as I left the hotel. The mid-70 degree weather feels good on my skin. Remembering the mountains of New England snow back home, I welcome this mild warmth in the February air.

The vendors who arrive each day on the boardwalk are setting up their wares and unloading their assorted goods. Their hustle and bustle in the quiet of the morning makes this little piece of heaven come alive with customers who, like me, look for bargains.

Despite all of this activity, nothing interrupts my quiet thoughts. As I walk, I wonder how in the world I have gotten here. Simply put, an apocalypse occurred. I lost my old life and am at this moment living a different life that has very little in common with my past except that I still teach second grade.

As I think of my second graders back in the school where I teach in Connecticut, I gaze out at the hazy sky that makes the Pacific look both surreal and majestic and worry if they will remember to hand in their home-school journals. I can't remember if I left a reminder for the substitute teacher. Funny how our memories don't hold onto the little details once we're beyond fifty. They are probably scrambling about in the cubby room, packing up their backpacks, getting ready to wait for their buses, and smiling out from under their hooded winter coats looking like stuffed munchkins. I'm hoping the lesson plans I left have kept their fidgetiness in check and that my students – and their substitute teacher – are content. With them in one time zone and me in another it's sort of like having a crystal ball – I get to look ahead while remaining three hours behind.

In my life today, I have a little hop in my step, and in my life back home, I walk in a dream, careful to dodge memories that continually rip at my heart. And you'd better believe I find memories everywhere I turn – from the front porch of my home to the innards of my bathroom vanity there are relics of the past. Old containers of every type of de-frizz gel known to woman are mixed among the countless bottles of nail polish varying in shades from Color Me Pink to Bogotá Berry Red, indispensable items for a 24-year-old, nothing for a 50-something mom, but still things that I can't part with.

I feel as if I've run away, but at the same time I feel as though I'm running toward something. I can't put a name to it. It just feels so good to be right here. Maybe it is the feeling of escape that intoxicates me the most. I don't mean escaping from my adorable second graders, but escaping from that alternating pain and numbness that have engulfed my existence for the last eight years and nine months.

How did I end up in this spot at this moment in time? Why have I been picked to receive the honor that is to be bestowed upon me tonight? I like to think that it is because of the intensity of the love I still feel for my only child who was swept away from me and has left a hole the size of the Grand Canyon where my heart used to be. That hole needed filling badly. Today it is being filled with joy, a feeling that I haven't experienced in almost nine years.

This chapter of my life seems to be proving Newton's third law of motion – for every action there is an equal and opposite reaction. Daily, I am amazed that the reaction is so positive, so compassionate and so strong. Everywhere I turn there are friends and strangers who know exactly what to do to get me through.

I've come to understand that the way we respond to tragedy and grief either buries us or brings out a strength that erupts from our inner depths that we didn't know we possessed. If that strength happens to attract the compassion of others, it multiplies exponentially and allows us to rise above the destruction and take on the world once again. Luckily, for me, I had learned early on to remain open to the gifts of compassion and love that surrounded me. Instinctively, my inner compass had always pointed toward the light, a result of being the oldest of three in a close-knit family that always saw the pot of gold just around the bend, no matter what the "crisis du jour."

The sun is now directly overhead, so I peel off

my sweater and let my bare arms feel that warm California sunshine. Loaded down with my typical "finds" – necklaces, earrings, and faux silk scarves – I begin to hurry back to my room at the Fairmont Miramar on the beach in Santa Monica and get ready for my big night.

My steps quicken as nervousness begins to take control and I think of the speech I have practiced incessantly – for days, weeks, and months. I run through it one more time, whispering the words aloud as passersby glance at this odd, middle-aged woman who appears to be talking to herself. I'm not embarrassed by their stares. I'm too focused to care.

Having made sure to leave plenty of time to experience all of the luxuries this five-star hotel has to offer, I enter my room and find a gift sent from my hostess for the evening ahead – a silver tray laden with fruit, chocolates, and Cabécou cheese. (You haven't lived until you've eaten Cabécou.) I restrain myself, only taking a nibble, worried that by indulging too much in this luscious delicacy, my streamlined dress will be ruined by little speed bumps of fat.

I run the hot water in the whirlpool bath and chuckle as I glance at the telephone and television built right into the marble walls of this palatial bathroom. I can't believe I've been given this luxurious gift for one magical day. I lie back and resist my impulse to pinch myself, overcome by a palpable feeling of awe.

I close my eyes and I seize this quiet moment to reflect on my only child, Andréa. I slide back and rest my head on the plush pillow propped alongside the tub and her happy face with those sparkling bright blue eyes, topped off with a tumult of blonde curls, comes into view.

I smile as I remember being told that she had once tap-danced her way through an entire math lesson. In her first year of teaching she'd been asked to fill in for another special education teacher on short notice. Since it was Monday, she had just returned from her regular weekend trip to New York City for dance classes at the Broadway Dance Center, and her tap shoes remained in the back seat of her car buried under her binders full of paperwork and CD cases. Knowing she'd need something extra special to keep the restless group in check, the tap shoes did the trick. The six-year-olds didn't make a sound as she tap-danced through the first lesson, bobbing her head back and forth for good measure, just in case there was a wandering eye among the antsy group.

When I heard this story from one of her colleagues, I laughed but wasn't surprised. She had always been the ebullient and uninhibited dancer – dancing her way through the ups and downs of life.

She was anxious for me to meet the very special children who had captured her heart – so young and many in wheelchairs – and I'd been thrilled when she asked me to visit her classroom early one autumn day.

Surrounded by a circle of adorable children, Andréa sat in the center of the room, smiling that brilliant smile. She confidently directed me to a chair nearby. I felt like the novice in admiration of the expert. Sun poured through the large windows that ran the entire length of her classroom wall, casting light on the happy group on the floor. I beamed as I took in the personal touches she had added to the classroom since the morning I helped her to decorate, just before the first day of school (payback for all of the years she helped me to fill my bookshelves and bulletin boards).

Captivated by Andréa's genuine warmth, the children sat attentively. Her long blonde curls spilled forward as she reached out to share a puppet with a child who had only one arm.

Tousling his thick brown hair lovingly as his little misshapen lips puckered into a kiss, Andréa exclaimed, "Wonderful pucker, Brandon. That's my boy! Keep those lips working. You're doing a great job." Two more wide-eyed children arrived at the door. "Come in, kids. We've been waiting for you." A little boy in a wheelchair smiled cautiously as he pushed forward, enveloped in the warmth of Andréa's welcome.

Andréa's smile and humor and certainly her infectious giggle delighted her students, but none of this was as important as the compassion she offered, knowing too well their struggles and frustration. She easily recognized that helpless feeling of wanting to accomplish so much, yet completing so little. She knew from the deepest part of her heart how to console and help them to forge ahead, even when they might have wanted to simply give up.

* * *

Startled by the ring of the phone (not used to there being a phone in a bathroom), I resist awakening from this precious daydream. The front desk lets me know that "the car" will pick me up at 4:00 p.m.

This fantasy trip to Santa Monica has me feeling as though I may have found a way to take on the world one more time. All fear is gone. I've already faced my worst nightmare, so walking onto a stage should not make me nervous. I keep telling myself that. I keep envisioning that I will feel as though I am being lovingly guided into a magical life that has none of the constant pain and numbness attached to it. It's going to be brief, so I'd better savor every minute of it. But maybe, just maybe, it will bring a new beginning.

Lesson 1

Timing: dancing in time with the music

"In life as in dance: Grace glides on blistered feet."

~ Alice Abrams

February 1979

The rain and snow swirled into a blinding sheet of gray as we made the two-hour drive to New York City. Tim and I had left our Connecticut home at 8:00 a.m., squeezed ourselves into our VW bug, and headed down the thruway. The windshield wipers slapped back and forth, forming icy streaks on the glass. I alternated between keeping a watchful eye on the road and glancing back at Andréa with worry.

Our little bundle of pink, our beautiful rosy cheeked, chubby daughter, perched in her car seat, sat looking at us, wide-eyed and smiling her usual cherub smiles. Just a week before Andréa had run around the house with her friend, Molly, giddily dancing a toddler's gyrating dance to her favorite songs as they blared from the Fisher Price record player that she dragged around like a perpetual sidekick. At eighteen months, Andréa had her father's love of music and a natural gift for rhythm. She had been dancing, giggling, and joyful.

But on that frigid February day, Andréa had a noon appointment, and the destination was unspeakable. As Tim drove, his eyes stayed riveted to the glassy highway. My mind raced to find ways to keep calm. I consoled myself with the fact that she was too young to know that she was about to enter a place from which children sometimes didn't return. She didn't know what cancer was, nor that she had just been diagnosed with it.

Andréa was about to be admitted to Memorial Sloan-Kettering Cancer Center's pediatric ward – a world where babies cry in pain and parents lie sleepless on cots beside their children's beds, muffling their own tears and sobs, a place of many nightmares. How had cancer crept into our idyllic home in the woods and found our precious only child? Our young lives were about to be altered forever.

For the early years of our marriage we'd been safely snuggled in a red pine forest, down a half-mile long dirt driveway that became almost impossible to traverse in the winter. We lived among a group of families who shared a love of nature. Our cluster of homes with floor-to-ceiling glass walls sat closely together preserving the surrounding ninety acres of wooded land that bordered the crystal clear Salmon River. The winters were spent sledding down the snow-covered hills, skating on the little pond in the woods, or hiking to the river through paths lined with towering evergreens.

Luckily for me, I had a strong passion – children. Andréa was born a year after I opened the doors of the Children's Center, a small nursery school in a church setting. I would pack her up each day in a Snugli strapped to my chest and we went off to school together for the afternoon sessions. She would nap in her portable crib, always within arm's reach and slept soundly amid the din of active preschoolers.

Tim worked at the local marina and sail maker's shop in Essex, Connecticut, but spent his weekends cutting up fallen oaks and pines to feed our wood stove, our only source of heat. A house of sliding glass doors, wooden posts, and beams was not easy to keep warm, but we had eagerly chosen this rustic lifestyle – completely different than our urban upbringings near New York City. We shared dinners beside fireplaces at neighbor's homes and Andréa had plenty of playmates and babysitters. In the summer there were cookouts and "sing-alongs" beside a campfire with the older kids helping the young ones to learn the songs as Tim played on his guitar.

One night everything changed. We were sitting at the dinner table eating tuna noodle casserole – a mainstay in those early days of domesticity. A sudden aberration caught my eye and would mark the turning point in our soon to be "forever altered" lives. As Andréa reached for one last bite of her whole wheat noodles, I thought I saw her little hand tremble. My gaze zoomed in on her playful face. She seemed to be delighted by the taste of the grainy pasta, laughing as she swallowed. Holding my breath, I looked for another tremble or any other sign of something gone awry.

Already one of those mothers who worried over every sniffle, a trembling hand could put me into a tailspin. Instead, I did for the first time what I would learn to do many times over: I denied that it had happened. I shook my head in disbelief and decided I was surely seeing things. When I said to Tim, "Did you see that?" he convinced me that, as always, I imagined "the worst" and off he went to visit with friends.

As the night progressed, I sat alone with my toddler, watching her every move. Had she really looked overly startled when I turned on the vacuum cleaner after dinner? Did her eyes have a seemingly rapid movement when she looked at me? Was she losing her balance and falling down more than usual? With the naiveté of my twenty-eight years, I decided that maybe I was truly seeing things. Didn't kids get strange symptoms when they were coming down with a fever?

I finally called the pediatrician at 9:30 p.m. and reached the doctor on call. He calmly instructed me to observe her through the night and call back in the morning. I'm sure he thought the same thing most doctors think about young, inexperienced moms who jump at the slightest symptoms and unnecessarily come running with their babies to the pediatrician's office, each one certain her child is fatally ill.

My eyes were riveted on Andréa's face as I readied her for bed and she fell asleep peacefully, looking angelic in her pink pj's. But I was unable to move from her bedside. I phoned Tim and tried to explain what I thought I saw and convinced him to come home right away.

Andréa slept peacefully through the night while I lay in bed pulling the safety net of uncertainty over my head for as long as I could. As the dawn finally broke through the darkness of our room and Andréa awoke, my shroud of safety had begun to unroll from around me. I picked up the phone to call the pediatrician. The things I "thought I saw" I could no longer deny. Now they were visible to both Tim and me. I heard the words coming out of my mouth, but I was still not willing to accept them – hands seemed to shake, eyes seemed to dart side to side, balance seemed off, and loud noises startled her. Dr. Miller calmly said in that soothing way that doctors use to disguise their concern, that we should take Andréa directly to the neurologist's office at the local children's hospital. She'd go ahead and make the appointment so they'd be ready for us when we arrived. I hung up the phone and sprung into action gathering up the diapers, binky, sippy cup, Andréa's favorite Cheerio snacks, and her Bert and Ernie dolls. Instinctively, I knew we would need as many distractions as I could provide. I prayed all the way to the children's hospital. Little did I know that it would be a long time before we would return to our picture-perfect home in the woods.

Andréa was admitted to the hospital immediately. We answered countless questions, stressing the details that I clung to for reassurance: no complications at birth and a perfectly normal pregnancy. By the time the initial examinations were over, she could no longer stand or sit up and her hands waved aimlessly as she extended her reach. Her attempts to crawl left her flopped over on her side. I couldn't bear to see her like this. Panic set in, and I looked to every doctor and nurse for explanations and words of hope.

After putting Andréa through too many tests to count, the medical staff at the small children's hospital diagnosed her with encephalitis. They said a virus had settled on the part of the brain that controlled her motor coordination. It would run its course, and we could expect to go home by the end of the week. That was before an intern probed further, and another barrage of tests began. Test after test fed the fear that crippled me. I remained frozen at her bedside. I watched in horror as my child rapidly changed before my eyes and there was nothing that I could do to fix it.

Tim had been called away to work just before the nurses entered the hospital room to tell me to ready Andréa for an IVP X-ray. I carried her into a large, darkened room and dutifully followed the technician's directions to lay her down on a table beneath a monstrous looking machine. I sat helplessly as she strapped Andréa to a wooden board and inserted an intravenous needle into her little arm. Andréa tried to kick and flail, but the straps prevented her from moving.

Finally, she cried herself to sleep, exhausted and limp. I sat there alone in the dark. Did they have to strap her to a board? What were they so intent on finding? Trembling, I waited for someone to help us. It seemed like hours before a doctor entered the room, introduced himself, and sat at the head of the X-ray table while I leaned over and caressed Andréa's tiny body.

"We're not dealing with a virus." I heard him say the words tumor, chemotherapy, surgery. The rest I refused to hear.

I urged him to bring in my mother, Gloria, and sister, Jill, who anxiously sat in the waiting room. I needed them to hear what he had so curtly told me.

After they walked in, he went on to explain that this was cancer and we'd get the best care at a hospital that specialized in treating children with neuroblastoma. Stunned, we watched a nurse roll Andréa's gurney back to her room. I wanted to pretend this was a bad dream, but Jill's sobs were all too real.

In a fog, we found a phone booth and called my dad and Tim. Always looking for the light at the end of any tunnel, I could see only darkness. A wave of dread filled me at the thought of returning to Andréa's crib. I didn't know how to embrace her. A child with cancer seemed so fragile. How would I know what to do? Outside of her hospital room, I paused with my hand on the doorknob. I would be opening the door to a new and strange life – a life I didn't want. For those few moments I wanted to be able to stay put in my "old life" – a life without cancer.

The next day, we packed up our wrinkled clothes, all the natural foods we had accumulated over the course of a week at the hospital (an obvious mockery of our efforts to have a healthy child), the sippy cup, binky, and Bert and Ernie and got ready to go to New York. We had decided to be near our families, and New York City offered the top-rated hospital for Andréa's deadly disease.

As we left the hospital, the night nurse, who stood by my side during many sleepless nights had become my guardian angel. She promised me that her prayer group would pray for Andréa. We would need their prayers.

Valentine's Day 1979

As Tim pulled our car up to Memorial Sloan-Kettering Cancer Center's front door on York Avenue, my heart sank. Scooping Andréa into my arms I held her tight, as if to protect her from what was ahead. My parents were already waiting for us at the door to the main lobby. Their thirty-five minute trip from Long Island had gotten them there early and given them plenty of time to wait and wonder. My dad's face was drawn and gray. Forever the worrywart, now he really had reason to worry. His first and only grandchild had cancer.

In spite of all the natural foods, natural surroundings, and homemade existence that I'd provided for my firstborn, cancer in the form of neuroblastoma had found her and wrapped itself around her left kidney in the shape of a deadly tumor of nerve cells gone haywire. For reasons unknown to the doctors, this had resulted in her loss of motor coordination and balance so that she was no longer able to stand, crawl, or sit up.

Acute Cerebellar Ataxia was the diagnosis for the neurological symptoms. Opsoclonus-myoclonus was the term used to identify the unsteadiness and her jerky eye movements. The myelin sheath surrounding the nerve cells had been damaged. The neurologist in Connecticut had explained that the sheath, over time, would regenerate and repair itself. How much residual neurological damage there would be was uncertain. I hadn't wanted to ask too many questions for fear of the answers.

We approached the hospital's steely entrance, trembling from the agonizing fear and the harsh cold of the blustery February day. As Andréa's chubby hand reached for my face it aimlessly shook in the frigid air until I finally grabbed it and held tight in despair. What had happened to my child? It hurt to watch, as she had been robbed of all control over her tiny body. This would be only the first of many things my eyes couldn't bear to see.

We found our way to a tiny, drab cubicle on the main floor where we filled out endless stacks of paperwork. Relieved to be finished, we rushed through the main lobby, crowded with sad, tired faces and stepped onto a long escalator carrying us upward. I wanted to turn around and run. When we got to the top we squeezed into an elevator to take us to the fifth floor where all of the other sick children would be. We wouldn't be alone. We wouldn't be the only parents of a child with cancer. We would all be in the same boat, a morbid ship that I did not want to be on.

With my back pressed up against the elevator wall, I cautiously peered at those around me – doctors, visitors, relatives, and other desperate parents. As I looked at the doctors in front of me, I wondered whose lives they had helped that day. What grim diagnoses had they made? What did they know about my child's disease that I didn't know – that I didn't want to know?

I'd already become a keen reader of faces, always looking for the slightest trace of concern – a skill I'd quickly learned at the children's hospital in Connecticut, where so many well-meaning faces had tried to spare us from their alarm after reading the results of all of those tests. They knew how devastating the news would be.

Riding the interminable trip to the fifth floor of Memorial Sloan-Kettering Cancer Center, Tim looked distraught. I wondered which fellow passengers were parents like us. Which ones had a loved one taken from them? Why had we all landed in this place of life-altering drugs and machines?

Standing next to me was a young mother. Petite and attractive, with short red hair, she had an air of confidence about her, except for the lost look in her eyes. Probably not that much older than me, she stood protectively holding her baby boy. Her child's head was bald and, as if that wasn't enough of an insult to his beautiful little body, there were large red X's drawn on his skull. I looked away. Later, I found out that the red X's were the markings where radiation would enter his skull and hopefully penetrate his form of cancer. How could this young mother withstand the pain? I had a clutching feeling that I should take my child and run – run away from what I feared would happen to her here in the name of trying to make Andréa well.

The February sun was setting through the window as we entered Room 501. I hesitated as I saw the hospital crib. I couldn't bring myself to settle Andréa into it. That would be an admission that my child belonged in a pediatric cancer ward. My mom held her in her arms as I stood bewildered, taking in the harsh new reality. Tim and my dad, Vince, stood by anxiously. With February's daylight hours short, I felt a sad sort of kinship toward the cold gray days that would mirror and reflect the darkness in my heart. The antiseptic smell of the hospital brought with it images of all that we might endure while we were there. I pushed both the smell and the thoughts from my mind.

Noticing a second bed in the room, I realized that we would have to share our sorrow with another family. I knew that I would rather cry myself to sleep at night alone. But the soft, yellow glow given off by the lamp near the window somehow comforted me and made this foreign place seem a little less formidable. It actually brought much-needed warmth to this stark room – our unwanted home for the next several months.

The other bed held Carla, a girl in her teens, who suffered from leukemia. She lay motionless. I couldn't help but think that for all her suffering, losing her hair must have been the most painful thing of all for a teenage girl. Her father explained that after being in remission, the disease had returned, bringing her in for another round of chemotherapy. This jolt made me realize that cancer had no mercy and could come back again and again like a stalker determined to take its prey. Flashing ahead thirteen years, I blocked out the frightening thoughts that began to creep in about Andréa's future.

He joked with Carla, trying to get her to smile, adjusting her pillows, and lovingly tucking in her faded hospital blanket. Although he tried hard to remain upbeat and strong, his spirit seemed broken. His tired eyes were defeated – too many hopes deflated.

Peering out the window to the East River, I was startled when I realized a nurse had appeared at my side. Probably in her mid-50s, she had the kindest and most understanding blue eyes. Her light brown hair was streaked with gray, and she possessed an air of motherly wisdom. She looked like she might be trusted – that she could become a friend to help to guide me on this unexpected and unwanted journey.

Tears must have been brimming in my eyes because she paused from taking her notes and put her hand on mine and said, "I know. I'm a mother, too."

That did it. I had tried to be so strong, holding in all the emotion that wanted to come bursting out over these last seven miserable days. It all escaped in a loud sob as I couldn't help but think to myself, "Why my baby? Why my little girl? What did I do wrong? What could I have possibly done to have caused this to happen to my child?"

I actually believed that this awful betrayal of all my efforts to keep my child healthy and happy could somehow have been avoided.

February 15, 1979

I learned quickly that life in a pediatric cancer ward could be as close to "hell on earth" as one could get. Loving families stood by watching their children being pumped full of toxins. I was struck by how easily some had embraced the word "chemo." How could they give a nickname to something so horrifying? Conversations about deadly drug combinations surrounded me. They sounded similar to conversations that I had just weeks earlier with mothers in Andréa's playgroup about natural baby foods and vitamins, but somehow the ingredients had changed drastically. How had the parents within these walls become so accepting of this world? I wanted to escape from the innocent little lifeless bodies, bald heads, pale faces, sunken eyes, and incessant vomiting. I felt as if we were all being drawn into interminable agony, and there was no way out.

At night I lay on a narrow cot alongside Andréa's hospital crib while she slept soundly, undisturbed by the strange new surroundings. I was grateful for her easygoing nature. She remained calm, as I literally shivered with nerves and jolted from nightmares when I did manage to doze for minutes at a time.

A curtain had been drawn down the middle of our room to separate my cot from Carla's father's. His nightstand had wedged its way through the makeshift divider and I noticed the mouthwash bottle full of a golden brown liquid. It didn't look like Scope. I wondered if it was liquor. Surely, this might have been his only solace during the long winter nights spent in a pediatric cancer ward. Who could blame him? I could hear him on the phone whispering to his wife in distraught tones through the flimsy curtain that separated our hard, barrack-like cots.

Earlier in the day he shared his frustration with me and said the words that tore at my heart and made me crumble: "No one leaves here alive."

Those words, borne of bitterness, punctured a hole in any sense of hope that I had held out, like a needle thrust into a child's balloon. My heart ached – for Carla, for her father, and for all of us in what appeared to be a place of no return.

February 16, 1979

The sun shone through the hospital room window. I bolted upright on my cot. *Where am I? This must be a terrible dream.* In my twenty-eight young years, I had never seen the inside of a nightmare. Unknowingly and unappreciatively, I had lived a happy-go-lucky life, and now someone, something, had taken an ax and shattered my dreams. Could I possibly bear to sit by and watch my child suffer in the same way the other innocent children suffered around us? Would Andréa lead a life of constant pain, drugs, and hospital stays? I even dared to wonder if God shouldn't take her and spare her what seemed inevitable. Why would we be any more fortunate than the families I saw all around me? I lay curled up in a fetal position, next to my beautiful baby girl and prayed.

In my youthful and optimistic existence, I had believed that you made your own happiness and conversely, your own misery. By seeing the bright side of things, you'd live the bright side of life. Positive brings positive. This simple philosophy seemed to be my natural outlook. My instincts directed me to those who shared a similar view. Surrounding myself with uplifting friends fostered an enthusiasm for life and had me believing that I could overcome or avoid most obstacles. My philosophy was being put to the maximum test. I believed that with an iron will and a massive amount of love, I would actually turn this devastating nightmare around. I prayed perpetually and refused to consider that my child would be taken from me. Positive thinking, I had been certain, would be the cure.

But I couldn't deny that we had been thrown into a sea of fear, with no control over the rudder. I desperately looked for a way to navigate. Each morning I would wake with that same jolt, the same hope against hope that this was all a bad dream. Then I'd look at the rigid cot I was lying on, hear the early morning clatter of hospital sounds around me, and quickly turn to see my baby lying in that metal crib while a wave of dread made me sick to my core.

On our third day at Memorial Sloan-Kettering Cancer Center, I rose and gazed out onto York Avenue from our hospital room window while Andréa slept quietly. I watched another busy New York City day begin to bustle, while people scrambled for taxis and buses, rushing to their destinations in their everyday life. How dare they! My child had cancer.

My head whipped around when a team of doctors, as well as Tim, his mother, and my parents, appeared at the door of Room 501. Andréa awoke and I lifted her into my arms, while I stood there holding my breath in expectation. We had ridden a roller coaster of feelings, allowing ourselves to indulge in a good measure of denial. Maybe a mistake had been made at the hospital in Connecticut. It was so small and their equipment may not have been accurate. Desperately, we tried to find a way to affirm that our deepest fears were unfounded. We felt our false hopes slide out from under us as the team of doctors spoke in slow solemn sentences, being careful to avert our eyes. They confirmed the diagnosis made at the children's hospital and charted out the course we would follow. Surgery would be scheduled for the very next day.

"Will Andréa need chemotherapy?" I blurted out.

"We won't discuss it until the surgery is complete," the oncologist responded. Somehow I knew that no one escaped there without it.

February 17, 1979

After a sleepless night filled with tears and countless questions running through my head, I awoke in a fog with a sick feeling swooping in and consuming my entire being. The moment had come to make the long, slow descent in the elevator, down to the surgery floor, and hand our child over to the surgeons and nurses.

Time seemed to drag and we moved in slow motion, walking alongside the gurney, holding Andréa's hands tightly. We approached the wide doors at the end of the long corridor. They automatically swung open into a preparatory room outside the operating room. Andréa clung to me, sensing my apprehension. Against every maternal instinct to hold on and not let go, I handed Andréa over to a group of masked nurses. Thank God they had warm, smiling eyes.

I had a sense that I might be saying goodbye to Andréa forever. What if something went wrong? What if she didn't come back from surgery? I felt helpless and ashamed that I had handed her over without a fight. She smiled so sweetly and good-naturedly, attempting a little good-bye wave with her tiny fingers as they carried her off to the operating room. My chest tightened.

We spent the next hours with our family, pacing the halls of the pediatric ward and praying, making the typical bargains with God that one makes in desperate moments. I scanned the expressions of other parents outside their children's rooms. Some spoke with doctors, anxiously hoping for encouraging words. Some clutched one another, silently. Amidst all of this I searched for faces with signs of hope, faces that had received some good news. Surely there must be some happy endings in this world-renowned hospital.

If not, then, "Please God," I begged, "let us be the first."

As the hours crept on, I finally sat at the window next to Andréa's empty crib. The sun had already set and in the dusk below I could see the slowing pace of the city around us. Things had quieted down as if out of respect for what went on inside those walls. Our family had been pacing outside of Room 501 all afternoon. As my dad saw the surgeon approaching, he gasped. In a haze of fear, we all aligned ourselves in chairs alongside Andréa's empty crib – Tim, his mother, my parents, and me all in a row.

Dr. Johnson was her surgeon, a stately Australian probably in his sixties. His piercing blue eyes were filled with concern. His long, graying hair, and oversized white mustache surprised me – not the usual conservative appearance of a doctor. But when I heard the dignity and compassion in his voice, I hung onto every word and knew that we could trust him implicitly.

With his crisp Australian accent he explained, "We've removed a large one pound tumor, along with Andréa's left kidney. With the kidney we took her appendix and part of her adrenal gland. It was a clean surgery and all of the tumor was removed." He went on to explain that children can lead full, healthy lives with only one kidney as the remaining one would grow to the size of two and compensate easily.

His kind eyes were filled with understanding and he spoke with assurance as he said, "There will be six courses of chemotherapy to ensure that any stray cancer cell left behind will be abolished." He knew this wasn't what I wanted to hear. The warmth in his voice let me know that he cared deeply and wished his news were different. We all exchanged furtive glances filled with fear.

After he left, I sat frozen – no tears, no emotion. I couldn't speak, but the questions cascaded through my head. A healthy life? How would that ever be possible? Andréa had already lost her motor coordination and now chemotherapy would fill her with toxins. My mother hugged me and said I should cry. I could not. Numbness had crept in and taken over every part of my body – even my heart.

I thought back to Andréa at fourteen months old. She hadn't started to walk on her own yet. The pediatrician assured me that some children walk later than others. I had read so much on child development that I knew this to be true, but I should have looked into it. I had even asked the pediatrician about what appeared to be an unusually distended stomach. Again, I was told not to worry. Had I been in denial back then? Did I intuitively know something was wrong, yet blocked myself from believing it?

That very night, after Andréa had been returned to us from the recovery room, she slowly opened her eyes. I lay my face next to hers on the pillow where her golden curls rested.

As soon as she saw me she whispered, "Mommy."

I cried then. As my tears rolled onto her pillow, relief flooded over me. She seemed so comfortable and peaceful. The pain medications were working and Andréa fell back to sleep. Even with the IVs, bandages, and monitors, she somehow slept soundly. Tim and I, along with our parents, hovered over her bed watching each and every breath she took.

The head nurse on the evening shift walked into our room. She abruptly explained that she must roll Andréa onto her side so as to avoid congestion settling into her lungs. I asked if she could just wait until she had rested a bit. The nurse gave me a flat "no."

Carla's father looked on with bitterness in his eyes as he sat waiting for Carla to return from the lab where she'd been taken for emergency testing. Suddenly, he stood up as the nurse began to take over. "Let her sleep," he shouted, "She needs to sleep."

A hush fell over the room. We held our breath and prayed he wouldn't explode, although we secretly hoped she would listen to his plea.

She explained again why she had to move Andréa, who woke up sobbing as the nurse rolled her to one side and then the other. I wrapped my arms around her and tried to soothe her.

Infuriated by the nurse's insistence, Carla's father slammed his fist into the wall across the room. We jumped. An angry outburst was the last thing we needed during those fragile moments, but we knew he had spent too many sleepless nights watching his own daughter suffer and we forgave him for it. It became clear that the feeling of helplessness had taken its toll.

As we had expected, there would be no special dispensation from the horrors of chemotherapy for our child. I couldn't bring myself to accept this, as I saw it as a death sentence. When I asked about her chance of survival, they told me 60%. That seemed minimal to me considering the risks of the drugs themselves. We had already seen children dying as their blood counts plummeted from these lethal drugs. Would it be worth the risks of pumping toxins into my baby's body for only a 60% chance of survival?

February 19, 1979

My mother had been interested in alternative medicine long before it became accepted by the traditional medical community. She'd heard of a doctor in New York City who used natural methods to cure cancer.

We discussed the pros and cons. Tim and I decided to travel downtown to meet with the doctor ourselves. It was my first trip out of the confines of hospital walls in almost a week.

I felt dazed as I stepped into the sunlight and onto the city street. Just weeks before, we had hiked in the woods, rushed off to play groups, and discussed the best remedies for diaper rash. Now I was going out into the world as the mother of a child with cancer. How fast our lives had changed. Walking along with throngs of busy people, I felt as though I had begun to accept this awful sentence for my daughter. I was integrating it into my new life.

As we rode the bus to 34th Street, Tim held me close. Despair consumed me and left me weak and feeling overpowered. I realized I wasn't ready for the world outside. I felt disoriented in this new world.

Somehow we found the doctor's office in a small brownstone building, down a flight of dark, cold, cobblestone steps that led to a vast cavernous basement. The waiting room filled the entire basement, lined with benches crammed with sad, defeated faces. With no room for us to sit, we stood huddled with the others. Our wait would be at least two hours. The clock ticked slowly. One hour. Two and a half hours. Finally we left. It wasn't for lack of patience. Our reaction to the dark and dismal surroundings told us we couldn't stay. Would we really be able to trust a doctor who practiced medicine in a cold, dank basement? We decided we couldn't take the chance.

We returned to Memorial Sloan-Kettering disheartened, confused, and filled with a dreadful feel-

ing that somehow we had failed our daughter. Chemotherapy would begin the next day.

February 20, 1979

The long wait during surgery was heartwrenching,
but watching chemotherapy drip down a tube into our
baby's chubby arm made us feel as if we were guilty
accomplices in an atrocious crime. I don't know how
I restrained myself from ripping out the needle and
tubes. I had dutifully breastfed my child until the age
of one, then fed her the most natural food, much of
it home grown. And now I sat helplessly watching as
poisons were injected into her body. I fretfully wondered how this would alter her future health.

The love that surrounded Andréa each day
distracted her from the daily pain of IVs, X-rays, and
injections. Her grandparents, aunts, and uncles kept a
constant vigil. They showered her with toys and affection. One minute there would be tears from the pain
of blood being drawn and the next minute Andréa
would be laughing as they gave her daily doses of love
and joy.

Children can sense their parents' fear, but I
was thankful that Andréa, unlike older children in a
pediatric cancer ward, could be distracted. She didn't
ask questions I couldn't answer. I thanked God that
Andréa was protected from the agony of worry. The in-
nocence of her not knowing that she had a life-threatening disease was a gift I felt grateful for. I watched
the older patients and wondered how their parents
maintained a strong façade, no matter what the prognosis. I was in awe of how they dealt with their own

pain and at the same time kept their child's spirits up. Some of them had other children at home who needed them, and they must have felt torn in half. In the midst of this nightmare I continued to grasp for something to be grateful for.

After a continual vigil at Andréa's bedside through so many wintry days, there came a moment when the sun spread its warmth. My mother encouraged me to get outside for a few hours to escape from the daily agony. Andréa seemed to be handling her treatment well, the doctors were pleased with her progress, and glimmers of hope began to allow light into the darkness.

As I walked out those steely front doors and set foot on the pavement, the fresh air hit me in the face and caused me to recognize hints of my old self again. Walking down the street felt like a new skill in my new world, but after the first city block I began to feel the familiar optimism I could always count on during a good, long walk in the sunshine. That invincible instinct to find some good within all of the bad prevailed.

I meandered for over an hour and found myself walking in the garment district near West 39th Street. I stumbled upon a little shop that sold only children's bonnets. Handmade and perky, the pink bonnet I bought had ribbons and carefully stitched bows. I knew I'd need something to brighten the day when Andréa's curls would fall out one by one. The shop owner had no idea that this little bonnet served as a symbol of my acceptance and my fight. My child had cancer, and I had found one gift that could hide the hurtful insult of taking away her crown of golden curls. I returned to the hospital feeling relieved and a little bit stronger, knowing that I had accepted the challenge of being the mother of a child with cancer. There were ways to take back some control, even if it was only a little pink bonnet I could offer as our armor.

In between treatments, Tim, Andréa, and I went to live with my grandmother in her tiny apartment in Brooklyn, hoping that Andréa would be exposed to fewer germs in her quiet home. With her famous hugs, kisses, and love of cooking, she let us know that she was happy we were there and that she would take good care of us. She excitedly prepared her delicious Austrian dishes (being careful to leave out the spices, but including all the healthy vegetables that Andréa would thrive on) and allowed us to take over every inch of free space with playpen, toys, and baby paraphernalia in abundance. The three of us focused on Andréa, day and night. The pain we felt was deepened by the loss of each silken curl. Within a few short days we had helplessly watched as every beautiful strand fell out and left her bald.

The terror and fear that consumed me never relented. As each test and examination was administered, I held my breath. What would they find today? After experiencing all that we had seen, I knew one thing for certain – anything was possible. There was testimony all around me. Children die of cancer every day, and somehow I had to make sure that it didn't kill my child. Prayer and my strong belief in the power of positive thinking were all that I had. I never gave up hope, and I refused to listen to the stories with unhappy endings that swirled around me.

Suddenly, Andréa developed a slight rash on her belly, concerning her team of specialists. They felt the risk of continuing the final phase of chemotherapy might do more harm than good. After giving her three one-week courses of chemotherapy over three months, the doctors felt they had already gotten any stray cells and her prognosis was excellent. We had just been given the gift that we had prayed for. Andréa was going home for good. I ran to the nearest phone to call my parents. As the words left my lips, I felt caution surge through my body. How could we have escaped? But we had. God was good to us. I would remain a positive person and I would raise a positive and hopeful child. With hope in my own heart, and gratitude for every doctor and nurse at Memorial Sloan-Kettering Cancer Center, I made a silent promise that we would find ways to give back in exchange for all we had received.

Lessons I Learned:

- Hold onto hope. Even the slightest encouragement from the medical staff should be taken as a gift and savored. It builds strength for you to face tomorrow. Believe that your HOPE will become your reality.

- Ask questions, even if you feel as though you are "one of those parents" who worries too much. This is *your* loved one and your questions could lead to the best treatment and best possible outcome.

- See the gift in all of this. There is no closer bond than the one made between a parent and his or her child with cancer.

- Don't compare your child's case with that of others, as it will only distract you from concentrating on what you need to do to help, and it will also cause more worry.

- Stay open to the help and caring extended by friends. They want to feel useful, so don't worry about burdening them. Accept their offers to lighten your load, as they will become the support system that you will need going forward.

- Find the hospital that provides the best care for the disease and do everything you can to have your doctors use state of the art protocol. If possible, commute to the hospital that is most well known for its research and treatment of the disease. And then trust!

Reflections of a Child with Cancer

I am the one you stare at,
I am the one you pity,
I am the one who is unhealthy,
I am the one in the hospital,
I am the one you distance yourself from,
I am the one who makes you want to wash your hands,
I am the one suffering,
I am the one suffering,
I am the one with cancer.

Andréa Rizzo
Looking Back - 1997

Lesson 2

Relevé: Rising up on your toes

"Kids: they dance before they learn there is anything that isn't music."

~William Stafford

June 1979

We returned home to Connecticut four months after Andréa's surgery. Our family in New York had been our support system and it took all the courage we could muster to leave them. Good friends and neighbors awaited us. We ventured back into life tentatively. The nagging worry that the cancer might return could not be washed away.

I hovered over Andréa as her motor coordination was slow in coming back and she lost her balance and fell easily. Her cheerful disposition helped both of us. She'd fall down, get up, and try again without a tear.

But it hurt to watch her attempt to get the same words out that had been so clear and distinct just months before. She'd look at me with such urgency in her eyes as she tried to communicate. Her sweetness and resolve broke my heart and made me want to say the words for her – if only I had known what it was she wanted to say.

She determinedly tried to put together toys that she once mastered without help. Confused to have lost abilities that had once come so easily, she aimed to make the pieces fit. She never lost her patience though.

Our once carefree life was now structured by monthly trips to the oncologist and neurologist. We were now parents of a child being treated for cancer. Ongoing check-ups and tests kept me in a state of perpetual anxiety. I slept very little and prayed a lot.

As her second birthday approached, she still needed to be held, as her attempts to walk were wobbly at best. She'd tentatively toddle forward in her gingham pinafores while I'd hold her hand and carefully guide her unsteady footsteps. Sometimes it was easier to just prop her on my hip – especially if we were rushing out the door and needed to get moving quickly. "Please God," I'd pray. "Help me to be more patient. She needs a patient mother."

Her eyes no longer had the jerky movements that had made my heart stop during those first few days before her diagnosis and her hands didn't shake as she reached for what she wanted. We still didn't know if she would ever be completely *normal* again.

Casting their eyes downward, the doctors had explained gently, "Andréa might be disabled to some degree for the rest of her life. It's hard to know how much she'll regain. Chances that the cancer won't return are still only 60%." I refused to accept those words. I spent every waking (and sometimes sleeping) hour determined to beat the odds. My child would be the exception. My hope would not be shattered by statistics.

Shamefully, I realized that I was not going to

have an easy time accepting that Andréa would be different than the child she had been several months before. I couldn't let go of my picture perfect dream. The loss of normalcy was too much for my young mind to accept. I explained this to her doctors. One young intern wasn't ready for my response when she suggested, "Get her old baby walker out and let her try to move around the house in that. You know – the kind she can sit in, but the wheels will allow her to use her feet to push herself around independently."

"I can't," I blurted out. It would be an admission that Andréa was now a special child with special needs. The intern looked shocked. I felt ashamed.

Happy and normal became my unrelenting goals. I began a constant vigil, measuring her every move against what was perceived to be normal for a child her age. We spent hours together, placing balls in holes, building towers with blocks, singing songs, naming objects, looking at books...and dancing. Her good ol' Fisher Price record player was traded in for a cassette player. She determinedly placed her feet wide apart, pulling herself up with the help of a couch or chair so that she could at least wiggle to the music in a new kind of toddler dance. Wearing a fluffy, hot pink tutu slung low around her hips, she would become consumed by the music and the movement. Her playful dance became more freewheeling. Eventually, she let go. Laughing her belly laugh, she danced on her own once more. When that day came, tears slid down my cheeks.

Our home was full of handmade play equipment that Tim and I designed and placed over a soft, plush rug in case Andréa lost her balance and fell. The big wooden beams that braced our ceilings made it easy to hang a variety of creations. Spinning and balancing on a swing I had constructed (putting my macramé hobby to good use) with wooden rings to hold onto helped Andréa develop her balance and strength. She and her playmate Molly spent hours on that swing and eventually figured out how to flip their little feet through the rings and hang upside down.

They would twist the swing round and round and then let go as they spun until they were dizzy. Unexpectedly, the spinning somehow helped Andréa to regain her balance. Her visible improvement spurred me on. I knew I could do more to help her.

Happily, we resumed our idyllic life in that evergreen forest – only a little slower.

We were getting our "normal" lives back and I made sure that every day included something delightful. Hand in hand, Andréa and Molly toddled through the pine needles that surrounded our home, both with beautiful blonde curls (Andréa's had grown back even thicker, silkier, and more luscious than before). We crouched in the strawberry patch outside of our door (with berry juice dribbled all over Andréa's OshKosh overalls), picked blueberries in the field down the road, and gathered apples from the local orchard for homemade pies. Weekend trips to our favorite Rhode Island beach offered squishy sand to walk in – great practice for her balance and the perfect cushion each time she'd fall down. Splashing at the water's edge, she'd let out squeals of delight when the remains of a small wave would wash over her – a beach lover right from the start.

As time moved forward, we embraced every season and found joy in each day. At Christmastime there were cookies baked at Molly's home and gingerbread houses made in our kitchen. In the spring, the girls would help to plant our garden, taking each little seed I handed them and guiding the brown fleck into the tiny holes I'd dug in advance. Our neighbor, a potter by trade, helped Andréa to create her own little clay masterpieces in her pottery studio right next door to our house. "Look, look! For you, Mommy!" Andréa would exclaim as she handed me one precious pinch pot after another.

Monthly checkups in New York City dwindled to every three months. We would pack up and head for my parents' home in Franklin Square on Long Island, the town I'd grown up in. Andréa could get a steady dose of her loving grandparents, aunts, and uncles and off we would go to Memorial Sloan-Kettering Cancer Center with both fear and hope in our hearts.

Andréa's motor coordination and speech were improving rapidly. By age two and a half, she was walking on her own and receiving speech therapy through the local school system. Ever the people pleaser, she worked hard to form her sounds as we practiced at home each day. "I've come up with a great new exercise," I proudly told the speech therapist. I'd discovered that bubble gum (we temporarily lifted our junk food ban) proved to be a surprisingly helpful tool in reclaiming clear pronunciation. Chewing seemed to actually strengthen her tongue and mouth, helping her to have more control over her words.

She especially liked this form of therapy. "Whatever works!" her speech therapist grinned. I'd get excited about every new word she mastered, even if it wasn't quite as perfect as her speech therapist would have liked.

Watching her happily play, sing, and interact with her playmates assured me that we were on the right track. "I help, I help," was her typical response to her friends when they couldn't reach something. She wanted to be the one to help them, no matter how hard it might be for her to manage the task.

The gift hidden in all that we'd been through was the extraordinary bond that developed between Andréa and me. It was intensified because I wasn't sure if Tim wanted to have more children.

When I saw an ad for dance and creative movement classes for preschoolers, I quickly signed her up and at age three, she was enrolled in her first official dance class. I'd get a lump in my throat as I watched her dance in a mirrored dance studio, wearing her little pink leotard, pink tights, tiny ballet slippers, and a matching pale pink tutu. Her blonde curls were held up with a pink ribbon. The young teacher allowed parents to observe through a one-way mirror, making it easy for me to see the excitement written all over her beaming face. Andréa intently followed the teacher's directions to sway and leap. Her little feet tapped rhythmically as she felt the music begin to take hold of her body. Even if she lost her balance she would laugh at herself and jump right back into the simple turns and playful circles that three-year-olds love to make.

My eyes remained only on her. Could she keep up with the other kids? Did she seem lost amid the action? She held her own. Here in this brightly lit studio, Andréa could transform feelings into movements that brought a proud glow to her face. She was in her element. I swallowed my tears. In that moment, I knew she would thrive and overcome whatever came across her life's path. Dance would be the key.

For all of the stumbling and awkwardness still to overcome, dance was giving Andréa back her balance and, most importantly, her confidence. Dance became the best form of therapy for her mind, body, and happy little soul. Simply put, dance made her heart sing. Before we knew it, dance classes became a regular part of every week.

By the time kindergarten started, all signs of neurological difficulty were minimal. I kept repeating in my mind the words the doctors had said so tentatively during those first exams. "The myelin sheath surrounding the nerve cells could repair itself and her balance could be regained." It was happening before my eyes. She walked fine, but she could fall easily on uneven surfaces. Walking in our pine forest with gravel paths was tough, but the challenge helped her eventually gain complete control over her balance. Her speech was a little choppy and some words came out slowly, but with her outgoing disposition she made friends easily and was an eager kindergartener.

But with kindergarten came testing. With testing came special education and at that time special education meant special classes. Andréa was pulled out of her regular class for two hours of each day, and of course this was a sure sign to herself and her classmates that she was different.

We had long meetings to develop her Individualized Education Plan (IEP). There were labels and the stigma attached to those labels: learning disabled, speech impaired – the list went on and on. I willingly took on my new role as her advocate and nightly tutor. Scissors, paste, index cards, colored markers, and boxes of teaching supplies covered our dining room table.

"Let's try a game with these words, Dréa," I'd say, using her nickname in my most encouraging voice.

"OK!" "Let's do it!" Andréa would willingly indulge my best efforts to turn drill and practice into play.

Having just landed a job in the same school Andréa attended, I was teaching first grade in the classroom right next to hers at Memorial School. It was a difficult spot to be in – both parent and teacher within the same building. My first responsibility was to advocate for my child, but that meant confronting my new colleagues – a delicate balancing act.

When Andréa was seven years old, her Special Education teacher tried to prepare me for what was ahead as she gently said, "When content areas like Social Studies and Science are introduced, with so many facts to be understood, she'll fall far behind the other children due to language processing difficulties."

Her words only made me more determined to prove she was mistaken. I knew in my heart that Andréa could do the work, but it was hard for her to process information and then express herself as quickly as the other children. At meeting after meeting, I heard myself repeat, "Why can't her individual needs be met with the help of a Special Education teacher included in her regular education classroom?" My concerns fell on deaf ears. Including special services within the regular education classroom was not typical practice in the early eighties.

On a late spring afternoon, we ventured to the schoolyard where a slope of green grass provided soft padding for her first ride without training wheels on her two-wheeler. I literally jumped up and down as she rode downhill on her own. Her hoots, shouts, and giggles were only matched by my loud cheers from behind. Seven years old and riding a two-wheeler on her own! Right on target!

When third grade began, Tim worked late nights so Andréa and I became a study team. Each night of every school day, we plugged away, reviewing and preparing so that she did not feel, in her own words, "dumb."

Constantly torn between my teacher instinct to help Andréa and my maternal instinct to hang back and let her do it all on her own, I wondered whether I was expecting too much. When her neurologist at Memorial Sloan-Kettering said, "Don't turn her into an over-achiever," I was hurt. But with her eagerness to learn, I decided that the tears she was shedding over feeling *lost* were not necessary. We would work together. I would teach her to never say, "I can't." Together we would prove she could.

Hearing that a child in our town had suffered severe brain damage due to a very high fever, I signed us up to be a part of the army of volunteers who worked around the clock to "pattern" the two-year-old's movements. Her parents had decided that Delacato's Patterning Method would be the answer to helping their daughter regain control over her body. They needed help administering the rigorous exercise regimen it required. Andréa and I would go to their house each Tuesday afternoon after school. Standing at opposite sides of the exercise table we worked Amanda's arms and legs in unison, following the prescribed movements that were needed to learn to crawl. We did this over and over to help set the pattern back in Amanda's neurological pathways. Her parents were elated at any signs of progress and proud to show us what Amanda had learned when we arrived each week. By helping this young couple and their child, I'd found one small way of giving back for all we had been spared. Gratitude resided in my heart for the miracle of Andréa's good health.

Amanda's struggles struck a chord of deep compassion in Andréa's young heart. It also provided a way for me to explain to her how far she herself had come. She had struggled in the same way that Amanda struggled to sit, crawl, stand, and speak. Andréa stared in disbelief as I told her that she too had faced these same difficulties. "Dréa, you are a miracle," I said. At nine years old, she now had crystal clear insight into all she had accomplished. I could see the disbelief in her eyes turn to pride.

All traces of neurological difficulties were gone, but with each school year came new academic challenges. Andréa's sheer tenacity created a life built on determination. She never gave up as she painstakingly worked through the nightly demands of homework.

But like all kids, she didn't want to be different than her friends and by the time Andréa entered fifth grade, her toughest challenge remained the ostracism created by the daily humiliation of being sent to the Special Learning Center. The questions she asked daily tore at my heart and left us both frustrated. Leaning over the kitchen counter, dipping her finger with perfect aim into the waffle batter we prepared together every Saturday morning, she asked with a quizzical look in her eyes, "Why do I have to do extra work and go to a special room? Why do my friends get to take certain classes and I have to stay with the kids who fool around and distract me? Why is school so hard for me?" No amount of consoling or re-explaining her medical history seemed to make a difference or lift her spirits. Her frustration was becoming ever present.

As junior high approached, my happy, hardworking, hopeful child was crumbling under the academic and social pressures. Nightly, we sat on the floor with study cards surrounding us and she'd scrawl note after note in an attempt to make the facts stick.

"Mom, I know it and then it's gone," she would say with a baffled expression full of discouragement.

Wiping away her tears, I reassured her that

the most important thing was to just try her best. My efforts to make her laugh with stories of my own frustration with algebra and geometry didn't bring a smile. Her anguish forced me to think of new ways to turn her homework into achievable tasks.

In the dance studio, she was safe. She could dance as well as the next dancer and on some days, she outdid them. During one "Parent's Day" at dance school, her ballet teacher, Miss Sharon, demonstrated something new for her students – the classic chaînés. These were a series of rapid turns done in a straight line across the dance floor. Once the demonstration was finished, each student was given the chance to attempt these continuous turns while moving diagonally across the room from one corner to the other. The key to keep from falling off balance was to "spot" something on the wall straight ahead while the body continued through the turn. I knew this would be a tough test for any young dancer, much less one who had endured difficulties with her balance years earlier. I held my breath as Andréa stepped to the front of the line. With that same laser sharp drive I had watched her muster over so many years, she found her focus on the wall across the room, narrowed her eyes in palpable concentration, and she began to turn – careful to "spot" – and turn and turn again. As she reached the other end of the room, she leaped, let out a screech of amazement, and high-fived her fellow dancers. Exhaling with relief, I thanked God for the gift of dance.

Receiving the *Most Dedicated Dancer Award* at her dance recital in sixth grade brought Andréa to tears. I sat there in the audience choking back my own tears, watching her walk up the stairs and onto the stage with pride written all over her face. When dancing, she simply forgot all that bothered her about school and let dance work its magic on her self-esteem. She'd come alive with self-confidence as she tapped or leaped across the dance floor. At home, she'd slip on her black dance slippers, move the furniture in her room aside, and turn up the music. I could tell by the deafening noise coming from her bedroom that a sense of freedom had washed over her – freedom to express herself. Given the choice, she'd have gone to dance class every day.

It became obvious by sixth grade that the time needed for homework was increasing to the point that she would have to cut back on her dance classes. "I'm sorry honey. It's just too stressful. You need to simplify your week so you can get your homework done and have a good night's sleep." As those words slid from my lips I knew how unfair they were.

With junior high school came the toughest questions – questions I didn't have answers to. In the darkness of her bedroom, I sat at the edge of her bed and listened as she cried. "Please stay here and talk. I don't want to close my eyes and go to sleep. I'll have to go to school again when I open my eyes in the morning. I hate it there. Why do I always feel so dumb when I work so hard?"

I knew then and there that we had to do something different. Tim and I looked into private schools. Small classes in a nurturing and positive environment might bring back her waning confidence. The teachers would have time to give each individual child all they needed to grow and blossom into the person each was capable of becoming. We enrolled her in the Moorland Hill School. It was the best decision we ever made as parents. The coursework was more demanding and the standards were higher, but Andréa thrived because of the personal attention she received. Dancing, coupled with sports (a requirement at her new school) were outlets that boosted her confidence and made her entry into high school a smooth one.

With a love for all things goofy and a sense of humor that was contagious, she began Mercy High School sporting her trademark Elmo backpack and a classic Catholic school uniform. She'd made the field hockey team at the all-girl high school and after practice she'd walk into dance class in her plaid skirt and cleats and change into leotards and jazz shoes. She laughed loudly and loved deeply – and a young woman overflowing with confidence began to emerge.

Mercy High School was academically tough, but her early years of learning and re-learning had been a gift. She had developed the persistence she needed to tackle her coursework. I'd get a call from her each day during my lunchtime. "Mom, I'm staying after school for extra help. We have a test in math tomorrow. I'll be a couple of hours late." She wasn't afraid to ask for support. Her personal success was too important. She simply didn't care what others thought.

Whenever her schedule allowed, she'd come to my classroom to help out. She'd walk the mile from her bus stop in our town's center and then trudge up the hill to Memorial School. She'd immediately find the one child in my class who needed an extra hug or a reason to smile. With a soft and understanding voice she'd fill them with encouragement.

While working with severely disabled children at an Easter Seals Camp each summer, her desire to help those in need intensified. At the end of each hot day she'd come home gushing with stories, "Mom, you wouldn't believe what Keisha did today! She learned to cut with a special set of scissors the camp director found for her. She was so excited. She's never been able to cut her own paper before. She was laughing the whole time. I hugged her and she looked at me as if she had just done the most exciting thing imaginable. I wish you could have seen her." Andréa's eyes lit up with love as she described how she pushed Keisha's wheelchair into the main lobby and paraded around chanting, "Keisha can cut!" Andréa's life was enriched by helping these kids – her world transformed for the better. She had an uncanny ability to make children laugh and they loved her for her extraordinary compassion and zany zest for life. Knowing that her very existence was a special gift, she had no inhibitions about throwing up her arms, spinning in a spontaneous dance, and yelling at the top of her lungs, "I love life."

I pushed away haunting worries and celebrated life right along with Andréa.

Lessons I Learned

- Replace the sadness and frustration with joyful moments spent with friends and family. Ask questions of doctors, teachers, specialists, and school administrators. Don't take "no" for an answer when it comes to having your child's needs met.

- Be proactive! Read literature on your child's specific learning disability and know the laws that apply to children with special needs.

- Join parent support groups like Learning Disabilities Association of America and Special Education PTO groups as you will find strength from others' stories and feel less isolated.

- Appreciate the beauty of sheer effort. It will serve your child well in later years for they understand the rewards of hard work. Find the gifts that come through the challenges.

- Provide social experiences in your own home so that you can see for yourself how their speech and motor development compares to others their own age. This will make it easier for you to address and understand your child's teacher's concerns.

- Find their strengths and help them to pursue all that gives them confidence. For Andréa it was dance.

- Practice school skills at home, but if this proves frustrating for you and your child, hire a tutor. It will save you both from "fighting" over schoolwork and give you more time to do something enjoyable together.

- If your child is old enough to help another child who has more severe disabilities than their own, this is an opportunity for him or her to feel competent and needed.

- Create a "gratitude box." Suggest jotting down those things (no matter how small) that you and your child are grateful for. The box will fill and serve as a daily reminder of the gifts that come through a life challenge.

- Always assure them that they should never give up and that you have faith in their ability to succeed – but point out that success looks different for every person. Help them to hold onto their dreams!

Lesson 3

Pirouette: A complete turn of the body executed
on one leg

"I advise you to say your dream is possible and then overcome all inconveniences, ignore all the hassles, and take a running leap through the hoop, even if it is in flames."

~ Les Brown

September 1996

Like most parents of our generation, Tim and I enthusiastically helped Andréa search for the right college. We drove all over New England on weekends looking at one beautiful campus after another. "I really want to be a special education teacher," she said enthusiastically. "But I also want to dance. I have to dance!"

After attending countless open houses and listening to department heads explain the benefits of their programs, she had found everything she hoped for at Salve Regina University in Newport Rhode Island. It offered the same small, nurturing environment she had thrived in before. She soaked up all there was to learn about teaching young children with special needs and she danced with the university dance company. She had the time of her life.

There was a heart-stopping moment in her senior year, when Andréa announced that she was doing a comprehensive project on neuroblastoma for one of her courses.

"Why neuroblastoma, Dréa?" I asked incredulously.

"I want the chance to write about my feelings as a cancer survivor as well as what a child must feel like going through cancer treatment. I was too young to write those feelings then, but I can imagine what they were. I also want to research the disease and find out about the advances that have been made since my treatment almost twenty years ago."

Having requested her medical records from Memorial Sloan-Kettering to learn about her own surgery and her treatment, she ripped open the thick envelope of documents when it arrived. She read about the drugs she'd received and the internal organs removed – kidney, appendix, and part of her adrenal gland. She studied it until she'd memorized every detail and understood all that she had endured.

To top it off she wanted to include a video piece in her project. I quickly realized that this would mean going back to Memorial Sloan-Kettering Cancer Center to film the hospital room, halls, and playroom where she had spent those dreaded months so long ago. As I listened, I sucked in the moan that started edging its way up my vocal chords and my jaw dropped open.

"Will you go with me, Mom?"

I hesitated. How would she handle a visit there? Would she remember any of the trauma she'd experienced when she was so young? I knew I wasn't ready for a return trip, but her eyes shone with innocent enthusiasm as she waited for me to reply.

"Sure, honey. I'll go with you."

As we arrived at 72nd Street and York Avenue, my stomach tightened and my head began to swirl. I didn't want to enter those steely front doors. Although I'd be forever grateful for all they had done to save her life, I really never wanted to set foot in Memorial Sloan-Kettering Cancer Center again. I felt as though we had escaped.

As that massive escalator in the center of the lobby carried us upward at a painfully slow pace, I immediately felt the pangs of dread that struck me so many years ago. With the same fear and terror in my heart, I decided that the only way I was going to get through this day was to pretend I was somewhere else, some other hospital – and it would just be an hour or so before we were back out on the street.

But as we approached those ever-so-familiar elevators and the doors opened to take us to the fifth floor, my legs felt weak and my heart overflowed with dread. I hesitantly looked at all the faces surrounding us. Compassion and sympathy began to well up inside my heart. I wanted to hug each parent and tell them that this was my daughter and that she had survived cancer. I wanted to give them hope.

I led Andréa to Room 501. It was empty and dark. She hesitantly bent forward through the doorway and took a long look around as if searching for some clues that might shed light on what she'd experienced in this room. I watched as a confused look swept over her face. I backed away, keeping my distance. I didn't want to revisit those nightmarish days and nights. I didn't want to get too close.

We approached the playroom at the end of the hall. There were no children in sight and the social worker on duty allowed Andréa to videotape the little activity centers that filled this sunny room. She solemnly approached the play tables and colorful equipment and zoomed in on all that she could capture. Drawn to the bulletin board full of children's photos decorating an entire wall, she held the camera steady. These were the children fighting the battle she had fought so long ago.

"Mom, look at this little boy. He looks so sad. I hope his family is with him day and night. These kids need their families to cheer them up. I remember you told me that the only thing that made me smile was having my grandparents, aunts, and uncles visiting me and showering me with Sesame Street toys."

I stood there taking it all in – remembering how I appreciated the big, colorful flowers painted on the huge expansive windows. During my bleakest moments, they defied what was going on, down the hall, just around the bend. Their brilliance and whimsy had brightened many a depressing day.

Suddenly, Andréa burst into tears. "Mom, I can't believe I had cancer. I was one of these kids on the bulletin board. It must have been so hard for you and Dad. It was so many years ago, but I remember all of those checkups and how scared I felt every time we came back here – all those blood tests. The whole thing is still a part of me." I pulled her close as we stepped into a small foyer, and we both let the tears fall.

The young male social worker, who had been waiting for us to finish taping, dashed over. He listened sympathetically while Andréa shared her story with him. "I was treated here for neuroblastoma when I was a baby and was cured. My whole medical history just hit me in the face as I looked at the photos of those kids. I can't believe I went through what they are going through now."

She paused to catch her breath, and then looked him straight in the eyes. "It's impacted my whole life in so many ways. I'm just so grateful to be alive." She was saddened by the memories yet proud of her journey – her miracle.

We left in silence. Walking down York Avenue, Andréa told me about the research she had done and her plans to become a dance therapist. "I know the impact dance had on my life, and I want to help children with cancer and special education needs in the same way. I've already looked into course offerings at New York University. I want to work at Memorial Sloan-Kettering Cancer Center and give back to the hospital that saved my life." Her feelings of indebtedness had been ever present.

"How will you handle the inevitable pain?" I asked her. With her soft heart, she would be devastated if she ever lost a patient to this vicious disease.

"It's what I have to do," she replied. Through every bit of adversity she had faced, her strong spirit prevailed. I knew she would uplift and inspire each one of the lucky children she helped. She'd give them hope and love. Andréa would be a living example of how perseverance and a belief in a dream can move mountains. What a gift – both for Andréa and for them.

Andréa graduated from Salve Regina University on May 21, 2000, with a Bachelor of Science degree in Elementary Education and Special Education. For four years, she had worked intently on achieving her goal and squeezed in an additional teaching certification in Early Childhood Education, all the while maintaining better than the requisite 3.0 cumulative average and conquering the grueling tests required to become a teacher – and loving every minute of dancing with the college dance company.

In that huge tent overlooking Narragansett Bay, proud parents were everywhere. Flashing back, I saw myself sitting on the floor in our house in the woods with Andréa on my lap, watching her painstakingly put those blocks in those defiant holes. That very same persistence had brought us to this glorious day.

Bursting with pride, our entire family sat watching her graduate – tears flowing. When they called her name, Andréa walked up to the podium exuding poise and assurance with her long blonde curls tumbling down the back of her graduation robe. Her smile spread from ear to ear. This was the moment I had prayed for.

I looked up as one of her beloved professors approached me. Giving me a hug, he said, "I've never met anyone like Dréa before. She cares so deeply and is so passionate about life and her future. Such gumption! She will make a wonderful teacher. Congratulations. We will miss her so."

I couldn't utter a word for fear of sobbing right there in the middle of the crowd. I simply hugged him back.

I strained to find Andréa as the trumpets blared through the recessional. Hoping to catch the perfect photo, I squeezed down to the ropes near the front row as the graduates marched by. When Andréa caught my eye, her arm swooped up. Tears streaked her face as she waved at me and shouted, "I did it!"

Less than a month later on a steamy June day, I sat waiting impatiently in the car, keeping myself busy embroidering the last stitches on Andréa's photo quilt – a gift for her college graduation. The car windows had fogged up from the constant drizzle outside.

Looking up, I peered out and saw Andréa running toward me in the rain, hair drenched, smiling from ear to ear, and screaming at the top of her lungs, "I'm a teacher! I got the job!"

She had asked me to come along for support as she was interviewing for a position teaching severely disabled preschoolers and knew that she'd likely be facing a team of public school administrators as they barked questions looking for the most astute responses. I understood the anxiety that goes along with an interview, having gone through the same process myself years ago while in search of my own first teaching job. With college behind her and degree in hand, she'd spent months preparing her portfolio and long weeks sending out applications.

Always the dancer, she pirouetted over large puddles that pooled in front of the superintendent's office – arms waving in the air, hands full of paperwork. Jumping out of the car, I squeezed her tight to share this moment of triumph. Tears came to my eyes as I remembered the long road we had traveled to get to this point in time.

She bubbled over, giving me details of the interview and repeating again and again, "I can't believe it, Mom. I'm a teacher. They had so many applicants. It's only a one-year position to cover for a teacher who is out on maternity leave, but it's a start. I can't believe they picked me."

Looking deeply into her eyes, I said, "Of course they picked you, honey. They saw the fire in your heart to help those kids and they grabbed you! This job will be perfect. You'll have a small group of young children with very special needs." She wanted to help those with the most severe handicaps.

We made a quick stop at the teacher supply store to stock up on plenty of bulletin board trim and then set off to get the pencils, paper, and erasers that were on sale at Staples.

During a celebratory lunch at our favorite pizza joint, I listened with admiration as Andréa explained in her animated way all that she had told the hiring committee: She understood these children's needs so well because she herself had been in their shoes; she had overcome a debilitating disease as a very young child and faced the ensuing learning disabilities throughout her own school career; she wanted to begin her graduate course work in dance therapy. Through dance and movement, she hoped to inspire and develop her students' thinking, impacting the way they approached challenges, and fostering their confidence at the same time. During her months of student teaching she told me, "I actually feel their frustration, Mom, and my heart aches when I see that lost look in their eyes – a look I remember all too well."

I thought back to all of the sleepless nights of worry throughout Andréa's school years and wished that I had known then that this day would come.

I jumped at any invitation to visit her classroom. I was captivated. The walls were covered with bright posters of numbers, letters, and pictures. Photos of her students were everywhere. She'd personalized their books and posted directions with their photos making everything easy to identify. I immediately understood why she stayed so late at school each night. She'd put her heart and soul into making this a stimulating place for her very young students to learn and play each day.

I watched in awe at the effortless grace with which she engaged each of her students. She was standing in the middle of the group amid wheelchairs and an array of special seats to accommodate their disabled bodies. Singing loudly she began rhythmically moving, shaking, and pointing to each part of her body – then pointing to each of them to do the same. She'd turned their lesson into a dance. Her own joy was spilling over and the children followed right along. She seamlessly guided them from one activity to the next. Action filled the room. With affectionate hugs and tenderness she encouraged them to try things that may have seemed overwhelming. She kept repeating that familiar refrain, "You can do it!" She knew what it meant when someone said, "Yes! You can do it – whatever it is you want. Follow your hopes and dreams!" I saw it in her smile, in her tenderness, and in her open arms.

Proud that she had found her passion and been blessed with the natural talent and dedication required to make a difference in these special children's lives, I sat on a kid-sized plastic chair and took it all in like a mother hen. Filled with gratitude, I wondered how this could be the same person who struggled as a toddler with her own speech, could not balance long enough to take a step, and whose own hands shook wildly as she tried to direct her grasp.

I let my eyes wander around the room and noticed puzzles and blocks that reminded me of the ones Andréa played with for hours when she was a toddler trying to steady her little hands long enough to conquer each elusive task. My heart would break as I'd restrain myself from guiding my hand over hers. Now they were the tools that she used to teach others.

One night, after a long day of teaching, she came into my bedroom and sat at the edge of my bed. I was struggling with a questionnaire about the laws that applied to special education and asked, "What are the guidelines for identifying a student with Attention Deficit Disorder? Do they qualify for special services?

It seems like each year the guidelines change."

"Quite frankly it's one thing to look at the guidelines and another to see how each school deals with students who are diagnosed with ADD or ADHD," she immediately shot back. She went on to tell of cases she had observed and how frustrating it had been.

"It's best if you sit down with the Director of Special Education in your school system and ask them how they want to handle the case. It usually differs with each child's circumstances," she advised me.

Looking up at her, I saw my daughter as a fellow professional. This realization gave me a jolt. Somehow, no matter the age, we look at our children as "children." But at this moment, I was looking to my daughter for help with understanding the complexities of special education guidelines. She had grown to be a caring young educator. She was now teaching me.

Life had changed dramatically since the days of her early childhood. I had no idea how dramatically it would change again. Nothing could have prepared me for it.

Lessons I Learned

- Look for the gifts that have come from the struggles that you and your child have faced together: a special bond and shared gratitude for all that has been overcome. Strength and perseverance are true gifts.

- Help your child to use their talents to affirm all that they have overcome. Sit down and make a list of all of the possibilities with them so they can see it in black and white. One option might be: Share their story of triumph publicly or with friends so they can reach out to help others who encounter the same challenges.

- Whatever strengths they have discovered within themselves and talents that they enjoy, remind them of the importance of keeping those treasures as a part of their lives forever.

- Help them to hold onto their dreams.

Andréa's Feelings....

I sit here wondering...
If my life was never threatened
would I cherish every second?
Would I love the way I do?
I think I would, would you?

I sit here wondering...
If my life was never chanced
would you have felt me when I danced?
My soul which led my feet
to an unending spiritual beat.

I sit here wondering...
If my life was never dependent once on others
would I care, would I want to be there to love
and give to others?

I sit here wondering...

I think I would!

Susan and Andréa
at the Salmon River

Andréa after
Chemotherapy

Susan and Andréa at age 2

At East Beach,
Rhode Island

Andréa's
3rd birthday

Ready for
dance recital

Graduation
Mercy
High School, CT

College Years

Andréa and her dear friends
21st birthday party

Reflections

I am the one who dances,
I am the one who proved you wrong,
I am the one who is going to make it,
I am the one who will make a difference in children's
lives.
I am the one who is smiling!

Andréa Rizzo

Lesson 4

Brisé: a small beating step in which the movement is broken

"Adversity is like a strong wind. It tears away from us all but the things that cannot be torn, so that we see ourselves as we really are."

~ Arthur Golden

September 2001

Throughout the long summer of 2001, Tim and I lived at our summer place in Charlestown, Rhode Island, while Andréa attended NYU, taking graduate courses in dance therapy and dance classes at the Broadway Dance Center. I picked her up at the Westerly train station on Friday nights whenever she needed a reprieve from the stifling heat of the city. She was always glowing – hair in braids, wearing a bohemian outfit bought on one of her daily visits to Chinatown, dance bag slung over her shoulder, and usually holding a gift she'd picked up for me at one of her favorite shops in Soho. She exuded youthful satisfaction – a young woman with her dreams coming true.

With that laser sharp focus in full swing, she was passing tests and attending seminars to prepare to become licensed as a New York City public school teacher. The process was grueling, but she didn't seem to mind. She had her heart firmly set on a goal, and nothing was going to stand in her way.

She bounced into the front seat of the car. "I found an ad for a dance audition. It was uptown and when I got there I was surrounded by hundreds of other dancers. I've never been so nervous in my life. I made it to the second cut, but that was it."

Amazed by her pluck and "go for it" spirit, I asked if she'd been apprehensive about going alone.

"I was a wreck. I think they could see me shaking while I waited in line for the second round and knew I was too nervous to make it through a routine audition, no less an entire show."

"I'd be a complete wreck myself," I tried to console her. "What did you do afterwards? You must have been upset."

"I just went over to the Broadway Dance Center and told my sob story to my friends there. They all commiserated with me. They've been through it so many times themselves." She didn't appear too crushed – just content to have had another dance adventure in the city.

On Sunday, September 9th, Andréa packed up her Volvo (a gift we had indulged in for her college graduation, justifying the expense by the countless number of air bags the Volvo ads touted) and headed for her grandparents' home on Long Island to stay until a teaching job came through. Then she'd look for an apartment in New York City.

Excited about starting her new life, she called

my cell phone when she arrived. While we spoke, she filled the drawers and closets in my parents' spare room with the help of all of her young cousins who were excited that she'd be living so close by. She was thrilled to be near them too. She loved them like brothers and sisters. As they unloaded her clothes and myriad of shoes and accessories from the car, Andréa was anxiously waiting for a call from a family friend who was working hard to find her a teaching job as openings usually came up once the school year was about to begin.

On Tuesday, she awoke to her uncle's phone call inviting her to a Yankees game that evening. Always ready for a great time spent with my brother, Gary, she began to plan what to wear. But by 9:05 a.m. things changed drastically. Two passenger jets had been flown into the twin towers of the World Trade Center in New York and all hell had broken loose in the city.

Andréa sobbed on the other end of the line when I called her from my classroom in Connecticut during my 9:45 a.m. break. She cried for all the people in the World Trade Center – so close to where she had lived a mere four weeks prior while at NYU.

The New York City Public Schools closed that week. Hiring new teachers was the last thing on anyone's mind. Andréa was desperate for a job and still frantic with the sound of fighter jets overhead and threats on JFK Airport just minutes from my parent's home. I encouraged her to meet us at our Rhode Island condo the following weekend and with great trepidation, she drove north over the Throgs

Neck Bridge, careful not to look at the ugly void left in the New York City skyline and the smoke that rose from that smoldering grave.

She arrived in a state of confusion, emotionally distraught. She had a dream and now she didn't know if it would become reality.

Some friends told her she would be crazy to go back to New York; others said she was crazy to let fear stand in her way. Threats of anthrax attacks were constant and she would have to pass through Penn Station twice each day amid armored guards carrying machine guns if she commuted to whatever job she found.

"New York City is a target right now and things could get worse," I reasoned with her. "There are job openings in Rhode Island. You can live at the condo and teach in Rhode Island. Wait until next year to move to the city. You'll have time to see what happens there. Hopefully things will have calmed down by then." I wanted to protect her. I wanted her home... anywhere but New York City.

In the end she took my advice. How I regret giving it. If we each have a path to follow, I had encouraged Andréa to veer from hers.

One morning before school began, I had the television on in my classroom. We were all vigilant for updates about survivors and those lost. I hurried back from across the hall where I had been copying the tests I needed for the day. As I walked back into my classroom, I froze. Katie Couric was interviewing a young girl about the same age as Andréa. She was from Virginia but was helping out at Ground Zero. Katie asked her if her parents were upset with her decision to do this. The girl quickly responded, "No, they are proud of me and would never interfere with my dream."

The television was talking to ME! I wanted to call Andréa and let her know that I too supported her in following her dream – but by then, she'd found a job teaching special needs students in Narragansett, Rhode Island.

Forever, I will wonder if things would have turned out differently if she had stuck with her dream and stayed in New York.

January 2002

There are no words to describe the sense of anxious anticipation I felt as 2002 arrived. It was different from common restlessness. Restlessness usually comes with dissatisfaction or confusion over where your life is taking you. This was different. A combination of hope, wonder, and excitement stirred in my gut, but I didn't tell a soul about it for fear they would think I was crazed.

Each morning I awoke to the sound of the alarm clock and in one fluid motion, I hit the off button and grabbed the remote for the TV that was in the loft outside of my bedroom door. With Tim off at work, I had mornings to myself and I liked to ease into the day with the perky opening refrain of the *Today Show*. As I pushed myself out from under the covers, I felt that familiar sense of urgency and anticipation creep in, yet

I couldn't put my finger on what it meant. I envisioned newspaper and magazine coverage and even possibly television appearances. But, I had no idea why! Would it be the children's book I had begun? It was a simple story about snowmen, but with an adult message. The most resilient snowmen would survive an avalanche – a metaphor for the disasters that come our way. My belief in the power of positive thinking still prevailed after years of trials and tribulations. Or would it involve the book that Andréa insisted we begin about our journey together? Andréa hoped our story might inspire others who were traveling a similar path.

The coming change would involve the both of us, I felt. Why not? Watching the *Today Show* each morning and sometimes hearing stories of triumph, I felt that somehow our story was going to be told. Call it intuition, a premonition – a sixth sense.

Months passed, and the anxious anticipation did not subside. Foolishly standing in front of the floor-to-ceiling windows in my bedroom, I'd strain to see the heavens wherever blue sky peaked through the evergreens. I actually asked out loud what it was that I should pursue. I had a strong desire to go for it – whatever "it" was.

As the third month approached, I found myself unable to sleep at all. First there were days, then weeks of no sleep. I was falling asleep on my way to school, yet unable to sleep at night in my bed. In between were exhausting hours of teaching eager second graders.

Chamomile tea, warm milk, and meditation were among my nightly remedies. Still no sleep.

As tired as I was, I visited bookstores and scoured the shelves, intrigued by the stories of everyday life. I began to see how one person's story was another's inspiration and thought about how Andréa's and my book might do just that. One afternoon, an odd thing happened as I left the store. In the mall, I heard a young woman's voice call out, "Mom."

I spun my head around as I was sure it was Andréa's voice. How could it be? She was teaching in her classroom. I shrugged it off, but not without a fleeting thought of how traumatic it would be if ever I were to lose Andréa (I had never stopped worrying about her cancer returning) and how shocking it would be to hear a voice so much like hers if something had ever happened to her. Taking a deep breath, I scolded myself for my outlandish thoughts. Sleep deprivation can do strange things to an otherwise sane mind.

The anticipation coupled with sleeplessness created an ever-present uneasiness. I decided that the book must be the source of my anticipation. I began yet another chapter. Andréa and I would chat by phone and discuss how we could use our own experience to help others. We wondered whose hearts we could help to heal.

Sitting side by side on the beach one sweltering summer day, we cooled off while the water edged up and washed under our beach chairs. Andréa looked at me with a keen intensity in her eyes. "Mom, I know that if there had been a success story for me to read back when I was struggling in school, it would have given me something to hang on to. I've talked about it with my professor, Mary Connolly, and she thinks it's a great idea. How about this for a title? *My Teacher – A Mother and Daughter's Journey*." What do you think, Mom? We are both teachers. We have to do it!"

"We'll do it!" I agreed and then hugged her – my heart full of pride and wonder.

May 18, 2002

I'd written a typical list for a rainy weekend spent at our getaway in Rhode Island: groceries – dish soap, paper towels, cheese, yeast, flour, and milk. Scrawled on the back of the half sheet of paper was a plan for later that afternoon: exercise, dust, clean oven, check the sale at T.J. Maxx, and deliver gardening items ordered for our condo clean-up day. Still sleep deprived, I hoped to sneak in a nap at some point.

Tim was enjoying a rare weekend home since his current job had him spending half of each month on a tugboat that he operated in New York Harbor. He sat relaxing, reading the local Saturday newspaper as Andréa rushed in from an early morning session at the gym in a miasma of bath and body spritzers mixed with shampoo. She ran upstairs to her room announcing with eagerness in her voice, "I've got a million things to do before I leave for the city."

After landing her second teaching job in Rhode Island, she'd moved to our condo, making the most of her altered "dream plans." In the living room below, we could hear her busily cleaning her room (amazing what rainy days can inspire one to do) and putting away her laundry. Her plans for later that day included meeting a friend (a new male in her life) in New Haven and traveling by train to New York City for a dance performance at The Broadway Dance Center. But she was having a change of heart. "Why am I going to the city? It's raining. I hate the city in the rain."

"What time is the dance performance?" I asked.

"Not until 8:00 tonight."

And then I said the words I will regret forever: "Well, play it by ear, Dréa. It's supposed to clear up later this afternoon."

I could have just as easily said, "Oh, why don't you stay home and relax?"

But Tim and I had plans to go out to dinner that evening, and I didn't want her to be left home alone on a Saturday night. I hated it when Andréa felt lonely. Besides, she'd been looking forward to this performance by Jermaine Brown, one of the Broadway Dance Center's teachers.

The performance would end around 11:00 p.m. She planned to take the train back to Union Station in New Haven with her new friend Jonathan, drive to Michele's apartment to spend the night, and then get together for brunch with her high school friend Paige. Andréa wanted to get home early on Sunday afternoon so she'd have the day to prepare for her week of teaching.

I'd reacted with disapproval when she had told me her plan weeks before. It would put them on the road after 1:00 a.m. I feared that she might fall asleep at the wheel.

By noon I had worked my way through half of my humdrum list and as I ran out the door to my neighbors' I heard Andréa call down from upstairs, "Mom, where are you going?" I knew she liked to say goodbye when she was going off to the city, which normally included an overnight stay on the Upper East Side with her cousin Chrissy.

"What are your plans?"

"I'm not sure. I'm stopping at Michele's apartment in Connecticut. She's thinking of changing jobs and wants to talk it over with me before she goes to work. Jonathan's meeting me there at some point and then we'll probably leave for the city."

I held back my instinct to ask why she wouldn't reconsider her plans and stay at Chrissy's, fearing I'd sound like my "overprotective self." Instead, I asked, "Will you be here an hour from now? It'll take some time for me to sort through this gardening stuff with the neighbors. I think you might be gone by the time I get back."

From the time Andréa was old enough to drive I'd been reminding myself that I had to "let go." Proud of the independent young woman she'd become and happy to see her traveling by plane to foreign places much farther than relatively nearby New York City while juggling her life as a successful professional, I still worried. I also knew that she valued my advice at times like this. Why didn't I tell her to stay? Instead I forced a nonchalant response. "If I'm not here when you leave, be safe and keep me posted."

"Okay, I love you, Mom."

"I love you, too." I turned and walked out the door.

Tim and I arrived home unusually late from our night out. We'd had dinner and lingered at our favorite restaurant on the waterfront in South Kingstown, listening to the live music that we came to hear each weekend. Before we left we chatted with the restaurant manager and ended up getting home well after midnight.

As soon as we arrived back at the condo, I picked up the phone and began to dial Andréa's cell phone number. I stopped and looked at the clock: 12:45 a.m. – too late to call a 24-year-old who was out on a date. I should have called earlier, but time had gotten away from me. I reassured myself that at least I didn't have to worry about her as she was with a strong, protective male friend. I admonished myself, thinking, "Susan, you have got to let go."

Before going to sleep, I folded the outfits I had picked out for her on my shopping spree at T.J. Maxx and set them on her bed. A surprise for when she returned.

May 19, 2002

That life-changing knock on the door came at 5:30 a.m. on what I'd expected to be a sunny spring morning. It jolted me from the sound sleep that I had sought for months. The heavy rain had moved off the coast during the night and the dawn peeked through the bedroom window. Tim jumped up and with a grumble he rushed to the door.

Still in bed, I listened to grave, hushed voices below. In a stern tone, Tim demanded I come downstairs. He sounded angry. The groggy noise in my brain shifted from annoyed belligerence to a loud confusion. I couldn't imagine who would disturb us at this ungodly hour in the morning. Had someone stolen our car? Was there a break-in at the neighbor's?

As I got to the bottom of the stairs I could see Tim holding his head and then everything began to slow down. A pair of policemen stood with heads bowed in the pre-dawn shadows just inside the doorway. Still confused, I blanked when I heard Tim say the unthinkable words, "Susan, Andréa's been killed in a car accident." He said it very clearly, but my mind immediately began to do what it had learned to do before. It went into that familiar place of denial. The two officers stood there emotionless, looking like they couldn't wait to leave.

I shot back at Tim, "This can't be true. There must have been a mistake." I held my breath as I caught Tim questioning their description of a red Volvo in the Bronx. I jumped on that error like a mother tiger swatting away a predator. Andréa's Volvo was midnight blue. Clearly there had been a terrible mistake. Plus, she had taken the train to the city. She never took her car. She couldn't have been in the Bronx.

Anger began to well up inside me as these two intruders had carelessly walked through our door and with the slip of a few misguided words, seemed to be intent on destroying the core of our lives. I held out a thread of hope that they were confusing our beautiful, giggly, compassionate daughter who had a bigger-than-life personality with some other unfortunate person who had crossed the path of a drunk driver on the godforsaken Cross Bronx Expressway.

"Her car is midnight blue," I kept saying over and over, convincing myself that she would be home soon.

The policemen had accomplished their mission and walked out of our home as quickly and abruptly as they had stepped in. I collapsed on the couch and sat there frozen. Why were they leaving? Didn't they know we might need their hands to hold or their arms wrapped around us?

I kept saying over and over again, "The car in the accident was red and Andréa's is blue." Why wasn't Tim questioning that fact, the one and only fact that stood between the difference of life and death – the life and death of our only child?

Instead, he picked up the phone and called the morgue, the district attorney, the Bronx Police Department. Flat tire – holding the flashlight – about to get into the car – dead on impact. I only heard bits and pieces. I covered my ears. I put up a wall, as if I were observing a gut-wrenching movie and I could remain the viewer, as far back in the audience for as long as possible.

Tim gathered more facts as I still repeated what now became a chant and then a loud scream – "Her car is not red!" I felt numb. Somewhere in my psyche I decided that numbness was good.

We exchanged broken sentences. Who to call first? When to call them? I said we should wait until our families were up and not to wake them with this unspeakable news. There was still a possibility that the wrong information had been delivered to us. By now full of facts, phone numbers, and certainty, Tim was sure we had to let our families know. I sat in a rigid stillness while he dialed my sister's home in New York. My sister – a second mother to Andréa who showered her with gifts and made her feel like she was just another one of her own kids. My sister – who would listen to Andréa's ups and downs through high school and then college, no matter the time of night. My sister – who would now go down the street to tell my parents that their firstborn grandchild had been killed by a drunk driver.

I squeezed my hands more tightly over my ears when I heard Tim confirm that my brother, the loving uncle who had put so much joy into Andréa's cherished life, sharing "over the top" gifts – like front row seats for the Knicks or the Yankees – was now on his way to a morgue somewhere in the depths of the Bronx to identify her body. I wouldn't allow these visions into my brain.

Breathing felt impossible. I needed to escape the spot where we just received the words that spilled all over our beloved get-away like a toxic substance, leaving our lives in pieces scattered throughout every room. Shaking uncontrollably Tim and I couldn't drive, so we walked to the beach to pray, to catch our breath and to let this life-altering moment find its way into our reality. I wouldn't let myself cry because in so doing I would have accepted the truth that Andréa had, in fact, been killed. It was very much like those first moments, years earlier, when I was not about to accept that my child had cancer. I pulled that same parachute string that allowed me to float a while in the space between knowing and not knowing. I was sure the phone would ring and the police would confirm that they had made a mistake. I resisted the impulse to call Andréa's cell phone for fear of hearing dead silence on the other end.

As my feet touched the sand, I took deep breaths as we marched forward along East Beach, looking up at the heavens, searching for a sign or an answer. This was the magnificent place where Andréa had done so much of her best living – jumping the waves, frolicking through summers with playmates while building drippy sandcastles, racing to catch glimpses of spectacular sunrises and sunsets, and growing up to walk this shore with a beau or two. This treasured beach instantly became my sanctuary.

The crash of the waves and the diamond-like sparkles of sunlight on the water calmed my heart. The light of a new day broke through the clouds. I assured myself that God knew we were right there on the expansive stretch of sand in full view of his merciful gaze. He'd watch over Tim, myself, and Andréa (wherever she might be) in unison – holding each of us at the same time. I wanted to stay in this spot forever – somewhere between heaven and earth.

Approaching the water's edge I stared in disbelief. Strewn along the shoreline were literally hundreds of dead starfish. Starfish were not common in Rhode Island. I'd spent many a day searching the beach for them. On the rare occasion that I'd find the remains of any of these endearing creatures, I'd line them up along windowsills in rows that made them look as if they were holding hands.

Immediately, I started filling my pockets with starfish, careful not to break one of their rigid arms as if they were each a special gift from Andréa. Gathering them, I was certain they were a sign from my daughter letting me know she was still with me.

It wasn't until the phone call later that afternoon that I began to give up hope that Andréa was ever coming home again. Finally allowing myself to speak to her devastated friend, Jonathan, who had picked up her lifeless body from the dark death trap of the Cross Bronx Expressway, I was sick with panic as my hope began to drain through a jagged hole that erupted in my heart.

His tears and gasps, in between the uncontrollable sobs, were too much for my veil of denial to hold back the devastating truth.

I felt all life leak out of me and I let my faith in a heaven take over. I was shocked at how quickly I clutched to my religious beliefs, convinced that Andréa was in a better place and yet still with me in the deepest depths of my soul. It brought me immediate comfort. I grasped onto this conviction like someone having gone overboard, fingers slipping, clawing, and flailing for dear life, desperate not to drown in the vicious sea of grief.

May 20, 2002

Those first days spun in a blur. Family, friends, and neighbors brought food and offered shoulders to cry on. Tears flowed while a sickening anxiety took hold in the pit of my stomach and the center of my chest. More information came through. They had come over the George Washington Bridge, headed toward New England and were stuck in traffic. A car crept alongside of them on the crowded highway and the passenger pointed to Andréa's deflated tire. She pulled the car off to the side, behind large yellow barrels that lined a construction site. Andréa had been holding the flashlight while Jonathan fixed the flat tire. As Jonathan put the tire in the trunk, she grasped the door handle about to hop into the safety of all of those airbags. But not soon enough. The drunk driver struck her from behind. Head trauma. Dead on impact. She hadn't suffered. That was all I needed to know. That was all that mattered.

I did not want to know any of the specifics except for the answer to one question: Why had they driven and not taken the train? Jonathan simply said they didn't want to walk around the city in the rain. But that sounded unlike Andréa. Later, there were more explanations that made more sense. Jonathan had been late and they could get to the city faster by car. There was a stop to be made at his parents' home along the way. Finally, I had to let go of my bewilderment. What did it matter? The decision had been a fatal one.

I was anxious; Tim was wrapped up in anger – a toxic mix. I lay in Andréa's bed, day after day. Sunny days made me bitter. Sunsets taunted me and my memories were like knives that cut deep into my soul.

I stayed at the condo while Tim returned to his work on the tugboat. I closed the shades. I didn't answer the phone. Standing up was difficult; walking was worse. It felt like lead weights had been strapped to my feet.

I awoke each morning believing that any minute the phone would ring and I'd hear her happy, sweet voice say, "Hi, Mom, I love you." Each time the phone rang, I held my breath and hoped against hope.

I envisioned Andréa on that last rainy Saturday afternoon as she danced around while cleaning her bedroom, CD player blaring, wiggling to the music as she turned a chore into a dance. I was haunted by guilty questions. I wondered if she took her car because of the cost of the train ride and the cost of the cabs in the city. I wondered if I had given her a little extra money for the train, maybe just twenty dollars more, she wouldn't have taken her car.

I agonized over all the "what ifs." Why hadn't I told her more emphatically about the article in the newspaper that I had read only days before she left, stating the astronomical number of deaths that occurred roadside while changing flat tires. Why had I missed that life-saving opportunity? And, of course, if only she'd stuck with her dream – not listening to her worried mother. If she'd stayed and lived in New York City, she wouldn't have been driving home that night.

One day, with time slipping away, I took Andréa's pajamas from under her pillow, where I had safely kept them and tucked them carefully into a Ziploc bag. Burying my nose in them and inhaling deeply, I smelled youthfulness mixed with the newest scent she had bought at the Gap just weeks earlier. I sealed the bag tightly, hoping to keep her presence alive forever.

But each new day seemed to take her farther from my reach.

June 2002

With Tim on the tugboat, I drove alone to Andréa's classroom at the Narragansett Elementary School to pick up the remains of her short-lived and ever so cherished career as a Special Education teacher.

As I parked in front of the main entrance, a group of her fellow teachers, mostly women my age, awaited my arrival. They realized what I did not – this would be a heartbreaking job and a mission too hard to accomplish by myself. We walked toward the office and my eyes caught a glimpse of the long, gray, steel cart, crammed with boxes and shopping bags holding every last precious item Andréa had lovingly picked out to teach her young students. It took my breath away to see all of her hopes and dreams piled up on a flat steel bed. As this vision burned into my depleted brain and aching heart I felt an arm slide around my shoulder. It was her beloved principal, Janice DeFrances, holding a basket full of spring flowers to distract me from the scene of another crime – the death of Andréa's lifelong goals and all of her promise.

We each dragged a box off the cart and walked in solemn silence. As we squeezed every precious item into my Jeep, it began to look more like a hearse than our summer beach-mobile. Every square inch was filled with my daughter's life for all to see and mourn.

I numbly accepted her friends' hugs and tears and drove back to the condo – the very same route that Andréa had driven at the end of each of her teaching days. I kept shaking my head as if I could shake away the truth. I tried to pretend that I was somewhere else, but I knew I was re-living Andréa's typical "end of day" routine and the pieces of her life were shoved in all around me in case I might try to deny it.

The sun was setting. This only made the moment more painful. Its golden light enhanced the beauty of the late spring day – one she would have loved. I opened the windows and inhaled deeply to breathe through the anxiety, the pain, and the memories. Miraculously, I made it home to the condo, slammed the Jeep door, walked up to her bedroom, threw myself onto her bed, and sobbed until I was limp. The room darkened and I welcomed the blackness as I slipped into a restless night's sleep.

The Jeep stayed full for days to come. I couldn't begin to put away the pieces of my daughter's shattered life.

June 3, 2002

I returned to teaching at the same school in Connecticut where I'd taught for nearly twenty years. It was much too soon. I had lost my entire life and two weeks later I went back to my classroom, commuting from Rhode Island as I couldn't face returning to our family home in the woods. There were only a few weeks left before summer vacation and Andréa would want me to be with my students, I thought. I had children with very special needs in my class and they needed me. One little boy in particular had captured Andréa's heart. She had met him at a class picnic I'd held prior to the beginning of that school year. He had Down's Syndrome and he'd made a lot of progress in one year. We were planning an end-of-year musical and his excitement over his part in the play had him bubbling over with exuberance for months. How could I disappoint him? Andréa wouldn't want that.

And so I cried all the way to school each morning, all through my lunch, and all the way home. I'd close my eyes as I approached the Gold Star Bridge in New London, daring myself to keep them closed in hopes that I might go over the side.

The play went on, school let out, and I collapsed.

August 20, 2002

As the wind rocked the sails of our beached catamaran, I lay on my back with my eyes closed. Tim and I were enshrouded in a heavy haze of confusion and grief since that despicable knock on the door weeks before. We had no words to offer each other – only a tense silence. Our marriage had been on shaky ground for several years. Tim's job had taken him away from us far too often and, with fishing trips in between, the distance between us had continued to widen. His anger toward the drunk driver was unceasing. I refused to allow anger to fester within, as I knew it would eat me alive. Grieving in ways that were completely different, we watched our marriage plummet.

As the water slapped the sides of the boat and I listened to the rattle of the rigging, I was reminded of our family vacations here on Ninigret Pond in Charlestown – summer after summer, sunrise after sunset, sailboats, and warm breezes. We treasured the beauty here in our favorite place on earth. As I wrapped my arms tightly around my padded, red nylon life jacket, I felt an unexpected comfort. I'd worn a life vest many times before, but as I hugged myself I was struck by the feeling of soft protection and much needed comfort.

With talk of a hurricane approaching, I shuddered inside. Andréa loved the excitement of an impending hurricane. How could she possibly not be here? I turned my head away from a flock of geese as they flew far off in the distance. They were headed south and I couldn't bear to look. Their v-shaped formation only reminded me that the season was about to change and that life marched on without Andréa.

The summer had been a beautiful one – one of those gloriously sunny and warm summers we would have shared and enjoyed to the fullest. I resented every bit of it. A day spent on our tiny sailboat brought its painful mix of emotions, but also provided a distraction. Working the sails and taking turns at the tiller, Tim and I avoided the tension that grew daily. It was our only escape.

I found myself doing so many erratic things to get through each day. I prayed that God would spare the mother of a child and take me. I closed my eyes as I would pass stores, streets, and whole towns that

Andréa and I frequented. I couldn't remove her happy voice from our answering machine. I wanted to be able to call our phone number and hear her perky greeting: "Hi! You have reached the Rizzo residence." I would not, could not, listen to the radio for fear I would hear a song that she loved. How could radio and television shows keep playing on as if nothing had changed? Didn't they know that my daughter had been killed?

The daily trips to the beach, both morning and night, gave me rare moments of solace. Looking out at the sea, a realization burst through the cloud I carried overhead. If things had been reversed – if I were the one who was in the heavens looking down at Andréa grieving for me – I would be shouting at the top of my lungs for her to be happy and go on with her life. It was a random thought, but it got me through the next few hours.

The end of summer brought the dreaded return to our Connecticut home. Walking back into our household of twenty-six years, a wave of reality drained the breath out of me. For the first time, I wasn't a mother in my own home. The protective nest we'd created, snuggled in the forest, full of fresh air and sunshine, was not the safe haven I had left just weeks ago. Did I belong here any longer?

Andréa's room, overflowing with clothing and makeup, leftovers from high school and then college, haunted me. Her favorite poem, Maya Angelou's *Phenomenal Woman*, written in her careful script, sat perched on the night table right next to her empty bed – a reminder of the strong spirited young woman she had become. A variety of dance shoes – from jazz to tap – were strewn on her closet floor, mixed in with her colorful array of beach flip flops. A quote from a Bob Marley song that her friend Paige had decoratively printed and framed for her for Christmas one year, hung on the wall over her night table dripping in irony: "In this great future we can't forget our past."

The scent of her bath and body spritzers, de-frizz shampoos, and mammoth collection of body lotions hit me in the face and left me breathing deeply with my arms outstretched as a crippling longing took hold. If I could have scooped the entire room into my arms, I would have.

Her dark green Laura Ashley towels with the cabbage rose trim that we'd picked out together months before were still hanging on the towel rack in her perfectly color-coordinated bathroom. She'd left them there that Thursday night when she'd come home to shower and dress for her friend Michele's birthday dinner – just forty-eight hours before she was killed. Although she worked and lived in Rhode Island, she'd driven to our Connecticut home that day, straight from teaching, to celebrate with her friend. She'd dressed and looked radiant in her black and white striped shell, jeans, and jacket – her favorite blue denim jacket that I would never see again. Her long blonde ringlets tousled about as she laughed and smiled brightly. I asked her to model her new outfit for Tim and remarked how gorgeous she looked. She was glowing. I wish I had said more. I wish I had let her know she had filled my life with so much joy. She was my reason for being, my purpose – from the time she was born, through years of romping in the woods and swimming in the peaceful Salmon River that bordered our land – until that moment when her enthusiastic radiance filled our home one last time.

August 29, 2002

I loaded my Jeep with prom gowns, music boxes, CD's, stuffed animals, tap shoes, baby ballet slippers, and high school yearbooks – the remnants of my daughter's precious life – and moved them and myself to our tiny condo in Rhode Island where I chose to escape from the memories of a family life that no longer existed. I discarded all of my old clothes (because they represented a life that had betrayed me) but was taking all of Andréa's precious things with me.

With what strength I had left I dragged myself into my doctor's office. Tears streaked my face as he wrote out a note for a three-month leave of absence from teaching. Although he wanted me to take six months off from school, I knew there would be several children with special needs in my class and they'd need their teacher. He also offered me the option of medication – anti-depressants. I declined. Why would I want to dull the pain? I couldn't just take a pill to make my grief go away. Thankfully, he understood.

In a daze, I crossed the street and entered a travel agent's office. Inside of an hour I had booked a cruise that would take me as far away from the holidays as I could possibly go. I couldn't bear to see, smell, or feel Christmas without Andréa. It was *our* holiday and we went over the top every year with decorating the tree, cookies, and gingerbread houses. "The Christmas Fairies" we called ourselves.

My last stop: the lawyer's office. I had visited him many months before the accident when I knew that Tim and I were headed for a divorce. Now was the time to finish that part of my life as well. There was no sense in prolonging the inevitable.

Losing weight rapidly, I lived what I called a peanut butter and jelly existence. It was the only thing that I could eat because Andréa didn't like it. Cooking and preparing meals at our condo in Rhode Island would remind me of happy family memories and the most basic form of nurturing. I no longer had a child to nurture so how could I cook? I couldn't go to the supermarket for fear of seeing all of her favorite foods lined up on shelves. Kashi boxes set off a panic attack amidst the cereal aisle – little reminders of the things she loved but could no longer enjoy. So how could I enjoy them? My food choices became ridiculously restricted.

September 2002

As autumn closed in, and the divorce process moved forward, Tim and I, accompanied by family and friends, made monthly trips to the Bronx Supreme Court House where the pre-trial of the drunk driver who killed Andréa was proceeding. I organized binders full of letters from those who knew and loved Andréa, expressing their sense of loss and imploring the court to put 57-year-old Carl Jackson behind bars. I gathered thousands of names, neatly listed on a petition that I hoped would further convince the court of his unforgivable guilt. We prayed the pre-trial hearings would decide his fate and avoid a full-scale trial complete with the excruciating details of a night filled with unbearable images.

Tim, mired in anger, was consumed with the court case and the drunk driver who struck Andréa and drove off with a hole in his windshield the size of her beautiful head. Carl Jackson kept going, but two couples in a car saw the tragedy unfold and chased him until he exited the highway where they used their car to block his, taking his keys and calling the police. We would never have known who killed Andréa were it not for these brave souls. Try as I might, I couldn't bring myself to meet them. I feared they might share with me what they saw. These were the details I couldn't allow myself to hear. I continued to keep my mind and heart in a protective shell. I could only write them letters to express my unending gratitude.

On March 19, 2003, the day Carl Jackson took his plea bargain, we filled the Bronx Supreme Courthouse with family and friends. The dark wooden walls, high ceilings, and worn leather seats were all too familiar to us. We sat in the front rows and I pressed my hands close to my ears, ready to block out horrifying details. Head trauma...dead on impact – definitive confirmation that Andréa had not suffered.

Propped against the railing in front of the judge were life-sized posters of Andréa. I had made them from photos: Andréa with Tim, myself, and her grandparents at her college graduation; Andréa in the center of her beloved young cousins giving them one of her famous bear hugs; Andréa in her classroom surrounded by her young, adoring students. I'd spent weeks preparing this display of Andréa's life to let everyone in that courtroom know just *who* Carl Jackson had taken from this world.

Through all of the pre-trial hearings Carl Jackson had expressed no remorse. I was about to let him know how sorry he should be. Frustrated that the court officers had placed him in front of the judge but with his back to me, I wouldn't get to look him in the eye. When the judge finally motioned for me to come up to the railing to give my victim's statement, I grabbed my notes and quickly pushed myself out of my seat without a moment's hesitation:

Your Honor, thank you for allowing me this opportunity to speak today and especially for holding firm to the three to nine year plea-bargain for Carl Jackson so that our family can feel that justice is being served. Will you allow Andréa's grandparents to stand beside Andréa's father and I, while I read my statement?

The judge nodded. I stood tall, cleared my voice to be sure that Carl Jackson would hear me and I plowed forward, trembling inside:

*Mr. Jackson, (*I held up a book of letters and an even larger book of petitions*), these books contain letters and hundreds of signatures from only a handful of the many people who grieve for the beautiful person you took from us. I've made copies for you in case you care to read them while you are in prison.*

Mr. Jackson these are pictures of our daughter, Andréa Susanne Rizzo:

-Born Aug 15, 1977
-24 years old
-Exuberant, loving & joyful
-Blonde hair, curly ringlets, blue eyes
-5'5 1/2 inches tall
-Big smile, full of laughter
-Childhood cancer survivor
-Loving 2nd grade Special Education teacher
-Graduate of Salve Regina University
-Accomplished Dancer
-Graduate Student at NYU
-The first-born grandchild to our family
-The first niece
-Beloved oldest cousin
-Much loved friend
-My only child

And behind me, Mr. Jackson, are Andréa's grandparents, aunts, uncles, cousins, and very dear friends. We all had hopes and dreams of sharing our lives with Andréa, an incredibly special person with an overwhelming love for her family and friends, and especially children. But that has all changed because you made a deliberate and premeditated decision to get in your car drunk on the night of May 19, 2002.

Mr. Jackson, when Andréa was only 18 months of age she was a cancer patient at Memorial Sloan-Kettering Cancer Center. All the family members that you see here watched over her tiny hospital bed, both day and night. When Andréa was old enough to understand the gift God had granted her – a second chance at life – she wanted to give back. She wanted to help others who had suffered as she had suffered. The best part is, Andréa knew how precious her life was. In her own words she writes, "I love life. I am so grateful to God and those who helped me to survive and succeed."

I could hear the sound of sobs around me, but I refused to take my gaze off Carl Jackson, determined not to leave out one last detail.

Mr. Jackson, Andréa was not just my child, she was my best friend. We were both second grade teachers. She had a great idea. Typical of Andréa. She wanted us to write a book together that would inspire others who may have struggled with cancer as she had. I was only able to read the beginning of our inspiring book at my daughter's funeral. Unfortunately Mr. Jackson, that book will now have a very different ending... a very sad one...because of you.

Andréa was a second grade Special Education teacher whose young students adored her. She wanted to teach children with the most severe handicaps. Mr. Jackson, imagine how devastated those young, needy children were the day they learned their beloved teacher was killed by a drunk driver and she was never coming back to them.

Mr. Jackson, can you imagine if a loved one of your own, the center of your life, had by the grace of God survived illness, only then to be killed by someone who recklessly chose to drink himself into a stupor, kill her, and leave her there to die on the Cross Bronx Expressway? How would you, Mr. Jackson and your children feel toward that person? What consequence would you expect them to pay? Nothing could be harsh enough, I'm sure. That is exactly how we feel toward you.

I paused for a second as I heard my voice

begin to quiver. Silence filled the courtroom and I pulled strength from some unknown place within my gut. I had to stay on track for fear of breaking down – diminished to a puddle of tears. I had to finish.

Mr. Jackson, you have taken away a bright, beautiful, and exceptional life from this world. You have ripped our only child from us and her family and friends are never going to get over it. The tears shed by her grandparents, aunts, uncles, and cousins are endless. The pain does not go away. Every May 19th we are going to reach back into our memory and pull out a devastating and horrific heartache. This May we will feel the tremendous hole in our family as we attend Andréa's closest cousin's graduation without our Andréa there with us. Every year on her birthday we will dread the pain of a day that was once an annual celebration of her very special life. For example, this year instead of a birthday party, we'll attend a mass in Andréa's name.

As for Andréa's father and me, we will forever hear the knock at the door at 5:30 in the morning and see the shadow of the two state troopers in our doorway. Every parent's worst nightmare. You created that nightmare for us and you had the nerve to ask this court to reduce your plea.

Tears were burning behind my eyes as I caught a glimpse of a court officer leave the room sobbing. But I had to keep my eyes trained on Carl Jackson. If I could maintain my concentration and a strong voice, I knew he would feel the impact of my words.

I have here news clippings about men who have been sent to jail for the following: 13 years for shooting someone in the leg, 18 years for smuggling drugs, 4 years in prison for using a false identity. You, Mr. Jackson, made a premeditated and deliberate decision to get drunk and drive that night. You crashed through large yellow construction barrels, killed my daughter, and kept on going. Do you really think that three to a maximum of nine years in prison is too much for recklessly killing a human being and driving away? Hopefully, the parole board will want justice to be served to the maximum degree. Hopefully, they will consider what I've said when you are up for parole.

Mr. Jackson, not only have you killed our daughter, you have destroyed our lives and killed our dreams. We have no future, nothing to look forward to – only dread. You have your children and you will enjoy grandchildren, too. But you have taken the life of our only child, the center of our lives, our flesh and blood and left her there on the road as you sped away on May 19, 2002.

Thankfully, Mr. Jackson, there were four very courageous people who valued human life and chased you down to prevent you from getting away with what you had just done. They physically kept you from continuing on a killing spree with your car. Who knows how many other lives they saved that night. How many more people would you have run down and then proclaimed again, "I didn't even realize it!" Thank God we have responsible and heroic people like this in our world today, to stop drunken drivers like you.

Mr. Jackson, our family, an incredibly close and loving family, has already received our sentence. A LIFE SENTENCE – of pain and grief, of loss and sorrow.

Here is a picture of our daughter's wedding. Here is a picture of our grandchildren. (I held up large blank poster boards to make my point.)

Mr. Jackson, there is no punishment great enough for you that will ever compare to the pain you've inflicted upon all of us. We will have to endure this pain for the rest our lives, without our Andréa.

When I finished my speech, I looked up as the judge appeared to wipe away a tear and Carl Jackson stood slumped with his back to me. No visible expression of regret.

The judge sat silent for several seconds as if he needed to summon the strength to speak. Finally, he quietly said there was nothing more he could add to the heartbreaking words of a grieving mother. Carl Jackson would serve three to nine years in prison for his crime.

We left the courtroom. Family and friends embraced and fell into each other's arms outside the huge wooden doors that closed behind us one last time. I firmly put Carl Jackson out of my mind. I wouldn't allow the poison of anger and bitterness to overtake my life. I had done all that I could.

In the end, Carl Jackson served only six years for drinking, driving, killing my daughter, and leaving the scene of her death with shards of windshield glass splattered all over his body. He was a well-behaved criminal who was rewarded with an early release from prison.

One month after his sentencing, almost to the day, Tim's and my divorce was finalized. A crucial step in my own healing – it was swift and amicable. After twenty-six years of marriage we were divorced within a year of losing our only child.

It's been said that the three greatest traumas are the loss of a loved one, divorce, and moving to a new home. I had experienced all three inside of a year, not through any willful decision of my own. I merely followed the dots.

Lessons I Learned

- One friend. Each day, I made sure that I could look forward to being with a friend for at least a few hours and preferably at the end of the day. I knew this would give me something to look forward to all day long. I did learn fast that if a friend came to my house, there would be the compounded feeling of loss when it came time for the friend to leave. I felt better visiting them at their homes or a restaurant so that I could walk away – and not undergo the pain of watching them leave and the deafening silence as the door closed behind them. I also made sure that I was with only one friend at a time so that I could control the conversation and keep it within the boundaries of what my heart could stand. Topics like children and grandchildren were off limits. With more than one other person at the table, I ran the risk of two well-meaning friends conversing together in front of me about their holiday plans with their children or their child's big win at the last field hockey game. I was clear about this with my friends. They knew what I could do and couldn't do. With infinite patience and understanding, they honored my restrictions.

- Books. Short books, even children's books with a "grown-up" message, can be a refuge and give your mind some nourishment. Many children's books have powerful messages hidden inside the pictures and large print. I read them over and over again as my weary mind was able to comprehend so little. Short books with encouraging messages of any kind are food for a wounded soul. Keep stacks of them on your nightstand. When you are ready to graduate to something more substantial, true stories of others' pain and suffering (biographies or autobiographies) will help you to gain perspective and feel the comfort of knowing that you are not the only one. A good book was like a good friend for me to look forward to being with each night. Some made me cry (tears help us to shed grief) and others gave me hope. I tried to end my nightly reading on a hopeful note and curl up and savor any clarity or comfort that I gleaned from the pages.

- Take walks. Movement clears the mind and calms that tight knot in your chest that builds until it feels like it may choke you. I found a friend to walk with each day of the weekend. Walking with a good listener is a bonus. This is one healthy thing that you can do for yourself (because you know that you aren't taking the best care of yourself). By the end of the walk you may have come to terms with at least one tiny piece of your grief.

- Holding onto hope. Finding ways to protect your heart is your quest each day, and you must do whatever it takes. I don't believe that denial is healthy, but looking at loss from many different vantage points can provide a lot of relief from the constant pain. I refused to believe that Andréa was gone – and sometimes I still do. I held onto my spiritual belief that we are never "gone" – we are just in another place – like heaven. Over and over again, I convinced myself that since Andréa was in a better place, I should be happy for her and not indulge in self-pity. I would think of the advantages I had in her being ever present and being able to talk to her in my prayers. I found "the silver lining" wherever I could within the dark cloud that had descended on my life. Some would call it denial – some would call it hope.

- Gratitude. Stop and savor the gratitude you feel when someone cares enough to brighten your day and lessen your burden with the smallest expression of concern or during those moments when you've completely broken down and a friend is there to pick you up. Pause to feel the kindness and love behind those intentions. It is a source of nourishment for your depleted mind, body, and soul. When you give thanks through words or cards it reinforces for that friend a feeling that they have been successful in filling you up – and that in turn fills them up – and a circle of love and caring evolves. Multiply that by the many friends and family members who extend their help, and your support system will carry you forward if you acknowledge its power and keep the circle open. I stocked up on stacks of inexpensive note cards and made sure that each person knew that they had made a difference in my life. I believe that my gratitude fueled their compassion and a circle of hope was ever present and grew daily. If you let them know how much their support means, they will continue to be there for you.

Lesson 5

Balancé: an alternation of balance

"The world is round and the place which seems like the end may also be the beginning."

~Ivy Baker Priest

As Christmas without Andréa approached, I had to run away. I couldn't bear the season that once brought such joy and now only brought overwhelming pain. Solitude seemed to be what I needed – solitude in a new environment devoid of memories. The cruise I booked seemed like the perfect gift for my torn and crushed spirit.

Worried about what my family would say and feel, I consulted a friend who had grieved the loss of her husband for many years. She put everything into perspective for me. "This is a time when you have to listen to your own heart, as broken as it is. Don't push yourself. There are ways to navigate your grief and if it means that you will make choices to do things differently, family and friends will give you carte blanche. You will have to find ways to create light for yourself at the end of the many dark tunnels that lay out before you. This is the window of time when no one will question your choices. How can they?"

Her advice helped me to manage every holiday or party invitation for years to come. I'd look deep inside and listen to my heart as I tried to imagine what each occasion might hold and weigh the cost of missing it with the price my heart would pay for attending. On that first trip, I was further reassured that I'd made the right decision when I learned that the ship's captain and my helpful bellboy were both named Andréa.

I awoke early on Christmas morning and climbed the countless stairs leading to the very top deck of the cruise ship as we docked in the harbor of Grenada in the West Indies. The pre-dawn light strained to shine through the overcast sky. Alone at the railing, surrounded by mountains poking their rounded tops through the clouds like giant green gumdrops, I stood silent and still as the sun began to rise and a brilliant and glorious rainbow emerged. Each color – deep indigo, turquoise blue bursting into a light green that became a sunny yellow surrounded by orange, then finally crimson red – created the beautiful wrapping of a gift sent directly from heaven. My heart filled with a mix of gratitude, excitement, and amazement. I was certain that Andréa was watching over me on that Christmas Day.

That afternoon I walked the crooked streets of the town of St. George's with an elderly British woman who had spotted a church steeple atop a cliff. Small but determined, she wanted desperately to visit a church on Christmas day, but she stared up the empty street afraid to climb the steep hill alone.

"Should we attempt to find our way up there?" I gently asked her.

"Oh, yes please. I'd be so grateful to have your help. Not sure if these old legs can make it," she replied with her distinctive accent.

Together, we climbed the hill to sit among the pews of the small, white wooden chapel overlooking the calm aquamarine sea. Our silent prayers were separate.

The occasional Christmas decorations seemed out of place in the Caribbean, so brash against the swaying palm trees and lush tropical flowers. Gold and red bows on wreaths seemed tacky. The sun's warmth and salt air were food for my spirit. Making the choice to spend my Christmas alone was a good decision and it would continue to be a central part of my new life.

Back home, it was difficult for friends to be with me at times. I couldn't discuss things that brought so much joy to others. Their joy was my pain. I didn't want to be included in conversations about their children – the same children who grew up with Andréa.

I learned early on that visiting with one friend at a time was all that I could handle. It allowed me to maneuver the conversation more easily if I felt it veering toward details I couldn't bear to hear. One night, I found myself sitting at a friend's home, relieved to have some quiet time with someone so full of understanding and sensitivity. Suddenly the kitchen door swung open and in walked her sister – stopping by for a surprise visit. I'd known her sister for years and was happy to see her. We exchanged hellos as she sat down at the dining room table to join us for a cup of tea. As any mother would do, she excitedly began talking about her daughter's new home. She quickly flipped open a picture album – one of those small plastic ones that most proud moms carry in their purse, ready for the chance to share their children's significant life events. She gushed over photos of her pregnant daughter with her husband – their new home, the Christmas tree in the background, and a gingerbread house on their laps with their toddler hugging them both. I tried to block it all out – tried to look the other way while forcing out the perfunctory ooohs and ahhhs.

Clearly, I couldn't hold back the hands of time or the natural evolution of life. Gradually, my dearest friends began planning weddings and showers. Most excruciating of all, they became grandparents.

My world was divided in two. People who had lost a child understood. I sought the comfort that comes when you find that you aren't the only one. But I knew no one who had lost their only child. When I did finally hear of one mother, I was told she had become an alcoholic and was in and out of rehab. I understood her desperation.

Then there were the people who had no idea what it meant to lose a child. I knew they were bewildered. I'm sure they wondered how I kept going – childless.

I'd always dealt with difficult situations by looking for solutions. Prior to this, I had stood in awe with deep compassion for other parents who had experienced such a devastating loss. I wondered how they continued on. This was now *my* problem to solve, and I couldn't see any possible solution, although I prayed for a miracle daily. Thirsty for hope, I'd write in my satin covered journal any signs of miracles that must be proof that Andréa was still with me. They were a daily comfort as I read and re-read each and every entry.

Just weeks after Andréa's death, a sparrow flew through the one and only sliding glass door of my condo when I had absentmindedly left it open for a few moments. It took me by surprise. Not once had a bird flown inside during all of the years that I'd lived in a house full of sliding glass doors in Connecticut. The bird perched among the baskets sitting above my kitchen cabinets. Leaning against the door jam between the kitchen and living room, I stared at the bird, who stared with intensity right back at me. We remained there in a standoff for what seemed like a half hour. Finally, I had to find my keys and get ready to leave for my weekly appointment with my grief counselor. The bird would not budge. As I waved my arms, swooping toward the glass slider, the sparrow just looked at me with a determined expression in its eyes. I began to feel a connection to this bird, as if it had visited for a reason.

Nervous that I'd be late, I left the sliding door open in hopes that the sparrow would fly out while I ran upstairs to collect my purse and sweatshirt. When I got back to the kitchen, the bird was gone. Before leaving, I got up on a step stool to look for it and felt around the baskets where it had sat just moments before. The sparrow was not there. Instead, my fingers grazed a ceramic bowl. As I slid the bowl off the cabinet I saw it was a long forgotten gift Andréa had hand painted for me during the days when she took pottery classes at the studio nearby. How had it ended up there with my basket collection? The words she had inscribed on the bottom came into view as I took it down – I LOVE YOU, MOM, Love, Dréa. The bird had brought me a message that I would hold deep within my heart.

On the outside, I looked normal, but I was locked away in my own world – like a sleepwalker going through the motions but not fully aware. I was busy, constantly on the move to keep anxiety from pulling me under. Every day was carefully structured to ensure I wasn't left without a reason to get out of bed. As busy as I kept myself, I was wrapped up in my own thoughts – visions of Andréa dancing, hearing her loud laughter, remembering her hugs – and trying desperately to block out everything that confirmed the world was spinning on without her. Stores were off limits as they inevitably played Andréa's favorite music and I would be forced to run out, loudly humming to myself to block out the painful refrains. The sound of a train whistle brought memories of picking Andréa up at one train station or another as she returned from dance classes in New York City. Several times a day, I covered my ears with my hands to block them out. I was protecting my heart and I didn't care how odd it might appear to outsiders.

School was the only place I felt I truly belonged. For the seven hours that I was in my classroom, I was the central person in someone else's life – my students' lives. At school, I still had that very positive piece of my old life with me. I could hear my voice speak with a happy lilt as I talked with the children. It set off a chain reaction transforming my insides from a confused mess of emotion into a reservoir of calm.

Sometimes, I would be startled to find myself in the middle of the day acting *normal*.

Had it not been for teaching, I would have spent my days lying in bed weeping and possibly even screaming at the unfairness of my situation. Instead, each morning I threw myself into the shower, rushed to get my clothes on, and then literally jumped into my car. The forward motion – just moving down the road – made me feel as though I could stay ahead of the anxiety and the grief. I had a long drive and it proved to be a time that I used for reflection and planning the day or hours ahead. Since I wasn't alone (there were other cars out there on the road with me), I was able to think about things that were sometimes too painful to face in the loneliness of my own home. As soon as I arrived at work, there was "people energy" around me. Fortunately, I was surrounded by positive people who truly let me know that they cared and checked in with a kind word or a gift throughout the day. Nightly phone calls from my sister kept me afloat. She shared my pain and got me through the hours when darkness caved in on me and anxiety took over.

Friends understood how hard it was to face the long weekends alone. Patti, Andréa's second and third grade teacher, had remained a friend and colleague. She shared a bond with Andréa right through her college years when Andréa would return to visit her, entering her classroom with arms wide open – ready to embrace her beloved teacher.

Every Friday afternoon when I pulled into the driveway, sad and exhausted, remembering how I'd looked forward to weekends in the past and fearing the emptiness of the weekend ahead, I'd open my mailbox and there would be a card from Patti. She knew just the right words to sustain me and give me a warm feeling inside, assuring me that someone cared deeply. For four years, there would be a card from Patti waiting for me every Friday afternoon.

The thoughtful deeds of friends kept me upright. A weekly invite for a quiet dinner with my dear friends, Rosanne and Michael or Karen and Mike, made the weekends bearable and once again, gave me something to look forward to. I ate at their homes, where I was safe from any reminders.

I gained strength from spending time with Andréa's girlfriends who continually called with invites for dinner or would make the trip to my home and we'd spend days on the beach reminiscing. When sitting with Melissa, Michele, Paige, Katie, Maire, Erin, and Lisa (the whole group, a team ready to listen to me at a moment's notice), I sensed a little bit of her within each of them. "Remember the time she rollerbladed over that drawbridge in Ft. Lauderdale on spring break? She didn't know that it had begun to open up at the top." They couldn't stop laughing as each one added another piece of the story.

"She made it to the bottom with just seconds to spare as she screamed out that loud high-pitched laugh of hers. We laughed so hard we cried."

Apparently, there were "tambourine playing Thursdays" in Newport.

"Oh, you should have seen Dréa dancing on stage with the guitar player as she pounded out the beat on a tambourine. Every Thursday! You know how she loved to be the center of attention." Since I hadn't been there for any of these antics (thankfully), I felt as if a new piece of my daughter's life was being revealed to me through her friends and I accepted every morsel like a brand new gift.

I remained in awe of these young women, way beyond their years in their ability to think of thoughtful deeds to express their love for their friend. Their phone calls and visits cheered me and reassured me that they hadn't forgotten Andréa and never would.

How would I face Mother's Days to come? My own mother understood that this was a day I would have to add to my long list of celebrations that were too difficult to endure. After spending the day by myself, the local florist arrived holding an enormous bouquet of sunflowers (Andréa's favorites), and a card tucked in between the blooms read "Happy Mother's Day, Love – from your girls." I cradled the bouquet and breathed a deep sigh, amazed by her friends' thoughtfulness. Mother's Day after Mother's Day, there would be a bouquet of sunflowers at my door with the same heartfelt note.

Although it was never discussed, I had an unspoken agreement with family and friends: I wouldn't fall apart or break down in tears if Andréa's name was spoken. I instinctively knew that this would alienate them – making them feel uncomfortable or responsible for having caused me more suffering. I also wanted them to feel as though they could bring up Andréa's name freely as my heart would brighten when we'd talk about her. As long as we could talk about her, she was still here – not forever gone – not forgotten.

Lessons I Learned

– Something to look forward to. Nights are the hardest and as the day fades to black, the anxiety, depression, anger, and a multitude of feelings that you've kept in check all day seem to completely unravel. I looked for ways to structure every day with places to go to that did not hold memories. I sought out new libraries and coffee shops with soothing lighting and quiet nooks to curl up and read or do paperwork. I was alone, but not alone within the deafening quiet of the four walls of my home. There were people around to distract me from my despair. Plans to meet with friends for dinner kept me eating (nutritional needs tend to fall by the wayside) and gave me something to look forward to. Even if my plan for a get-together with a friend was a few days off, I was able to hang on knowing that there would be a buoying of my spirit awaiting me later in the week.

– Protect your heart. Know yourself. Stay away from things that bring pain. If someone unknowingly has asked you to do something that you know will cause you pain (like going to a familiar place that you once enjoyed), feel free to say "no." Do only the things that bring relief. No one is going to question your new eccentricities. (They are probably wondering how you get out of bed to face each day.) With a brief explanation of how familiar things are still hard for you to face, the average person will understand. If they don't, then it is best to stay away from them as well. The idea is to keep the pain to a minimum so be careful not to put yourself in situations that are going to inflict further pain. That is not crazy – that is smart.

– Spend time with friends who can share memories of your loved one. It brings assurance that you are not the only one holding on to precious memories – and the memories seem to multiply when they are shared with others.

– Attend support groups like Compassionate Friends or have dinner with someone who has experienced a similar loss. You will feel less alone – less like you are "the only one."

- Create new traditions and rituals for yourself. Find just one thing that gives you something to look forward to and make it a part of your new life. For me, it was my "Get Away From Christmas" tradition. This is a gift that you can give to yourself. Find gifts wherever you can and shower yourself with them. A walk on a beach is a perfect gift.

- Go to work – sooner rather than later. The structure of getting up each morning for a reason outside of yourself is healthy for the mind, body, and spirit. Having to push yourself out from under the covers and pillows that you have clung to all night is the first step. It's not an easy one since your face is tear-stained and swollen, your head feels full of black fog and dread, and your heart is writhing in pain. As hard as it is, the alternative is bleaker and almost unbearable. A tight structure for each day that you've planned the night before will help you out of bed and into the world, even if you need to wear sunglasses to block out the glare of your harsh reality.

Times Square, NYC at 22 years of age

Lesson 6

Grand Jeté: a large leap forward

"Dancers know that the mind, body, and spirit are inextricably intertwined. The miraculous magic of expression overrides everything. It becomes everything. You are dancing with God. You are dancing with yourself. You are dancing in the light."

~ Shirley MacLaine

A colleague of Andréa's, Terry Schimmel, took the time to write me a beautiful letter that would eventually lift me out of desperation.

I read it at the start of another anxiety-filled weekend not long after Andréa's death. I'd awakened to a cloudy morning and drifted downstairs to the kitchen where I was greeted by a pile of mail on my kitchen counter – a mix of legal papers, bills, and cards from friends. I half-heartedly gathered them up, dragged myself upstairs, and flopped back down on Andréa's bed – where I spent most of my nights.

After sorting through the stack, I found the note from Terry. In it, she explained that she thought Andréa's memory should be honored by continuing her dream of helping children with cancer and special needs through dance therapy. Terry wondered if I'd like her to help me to form a foundation in Andréa's memory. I didn't quite know what a foundation was. I had no idea how we might begin to provide dance therapy for children. I didn't even know that much about dance therapy.

But this note would be my salvation. It touched my inner spirit, brought light into the darkness, and gave me purpose.

In those first moments of hope and optimism, I could have laid back down in bed, pulled the pillows over my head, and drowned in my grief. Or I could open myself up to the love contained in Terry's words. Somehow, I found the energy to rise out of my smothering pain and reach out toward the light. If I didn't turn this energy into something that honored my daughter then I had wasted a precious gift. I could create something that, although it wouldn't bring my daughter back, would keep her memory alive forever.

Terry's idea not only made sense to me, but it made sense to Andréa's many friends, colleagues and of course, her grandparents, aunts, uncles, and even her young cousins. Researching the steps to become a non-profit and then a 501(c)(3) tax exempt organization, required an endless stream of phone calls. We faced it all with a sense of urgency. We were keeping a piece of Andréa's life alive – her dream.

With little to no computer experience at the time, I relied on friends of friends who knew accountants and lawyers who had the patience of saints and were willing to answer my countless questions. This also kept any costs to a minimum since I was funding the preparation on my teacher's salary. Luckily my dad had the determination and the accounting know-how to work along with me.

Andréa had babysat for many years for a lawyer's children and he generously gave of his time, answering questions daily. With enthusiastic friends and family members helping me to tackle the mounds of paperwork, we finally had approval to begin fundraising, and then created a Board of Directors from among this dedicated group.

Through the long and complicated process, my family and friends, as well as Andréa's friends and colleagues, had found a new way to be with each other. We could talk, plan, share – and at the same time we felt we were doing something for Andréa. My parents, sister, brother, and their spouses provided me with a constant workforce – stuffing envelopes, collating packets, and asking their own friends' businesses to donate signs, stationery, and raffle tickets. My brother-in-law, Don, quickly organized a golf outing and my brother, Gary, set up a car raffle. Even Andréa's young cousins created adorable handmade hearts and dancers to sell at fundraising events and became experts at putting stamps on piles of envelopes. That helpless feeling began to lift.

Dinner meetings and breakfast meetings became a part of my new life. Andréa's friends filled my condo, anxious to share exciting fundraising ideas. As we stuffed more envelopes and designed logos, web pages, and brochures, our energy continued to build and laughter could be heard in my home again. I had found what would become my new *reason to be*. The knowledge that there would be new places and people for me to be with in new ways through the work of the Foundation would be my way of carrying on and re-entering the world. I had a gnawing desire to define myself (no longer a mother or a wife) and the work of a foundation might offer that chance.

Grief still consumed me, but a turning point

occurred. One long evening, after tossing and turning through unbearable dreams, I awoke in Andréa's bed in a pool of tears and sweat. I sobbed in anger over all Andréa had been robbed of after those many long years, months, days, and hours of hard work and endless persistence to turn every heartache and hurdle into a dream come true. I thrust my clenched fists into the bed and with every ounce of strength I had left, I let out a guttural moan and swore out loud to God and Andréa that nothing would stand in the way of our making her dream a reality. We would still be a team. Nothing would stop us. Not even death.

As days passed and the budding foundation began to take shape, a relentless energy kept driving me forward. Daily, I was amazed that those who surrounded me knew exactly what I needed to face each day. How could I possibly turn away from all of this love? It nurtured my heart and made me feel that I was not alone in my grief. Their wholehearted energy made my load a little bit lighter and more bearable. I breathed it in and hugged them with deep appreciation. Their love was like a salve for my wounds. The healing that had begun would never have had a chance to take place if I had shut them out and let my pain be a barrier between us. I felt that Andréa had sent these very special friends to me as angels on earth to guide me and hold me up. From all of the devastation emerged one beautiful expression of hope – the Andréa Rizzo Foundation – my saving grace.

My days were fueled by tiny miracles that would present themselves and open doors for me to walk through. Whatever was needed to help me achieve my newly defined goals arrived in the form of a generous person, a kind deed, or even what seemed like a sign from above.

A month before losing Andréa, I had attended a fashion show with a friend and her mother. We sat on folding chairs in a large tent amid women of all ages and there was a bustle of excitement in the early spring air. As the models prepared to walk the runway and the row of judges took their places at the foot of the stage to rate the most exquisite outfits, my friend pointed out, "That judge is the mother of the young girl in my town who was killed by a drunk driver two years ago."

From that point on I had difficulty focusing on the fashion show. I stared at the judge, in awe that she was able to talk, walk, and function although she had endured such a devastating tragedy. I never imagined that I would soon find myself sitting in her living room and listening to the vivid details of how she and her husband had begun a wonderful foundation in their daughter Katie's memory to educate young people about the deadly combination of drinking and driving. While we sat on their couch, drinking tea, and sharing our tragically similar stories, they took the time to share with me the reams of paperwork they'd created to start the foundation. There were press packets for their fundraising events, directions on how to set up a database, and countless helpful tips. They offered to assist me in learning the ins and outs of non-profit work and even arranged for the use of a local site for a future fundraiser. As I stood in the doorway of their home, laden with sample flyers, brochures, and press releases, they hugged me goodbye and said, "We really feel as though Katie's life shines on since the Katie DeCubellis Memorial Foundation helps kids and saves lives. Katie would want that."

John and Meg DeCubellis became my first beacons of hope. They had found new purpose by mustering every ounce of strength to ensure their daughter's life would still hold meaning. Katie was too special to be forgotten and, like Andréa, she always wanted to do for others. A foundation would keep Andréa's memory alive in a way she would be so proud of. Her name would be said, her story would be told, and most importantly her dream of helping children with special needs and cancer through dance therapy would live on.

A spark had been ignited and it was up to me to take on the challenge of making sure that my daughter's dream came true. I would not have to do this alone. Andréa's beloved dance teacher and dear family friend, Sharon Mulcahy, had recently become a registered dance/movement therapist. She made a day trip from her home in Connecticut to visit me in Rhode Island and we sat on stools around my kitchen counter. Sharon's eyes filled with tears when she spoke of Andréa as a young dancer in her dance school so many years ago. Sharon offered to provide dance/movement therapy for children with autism at the school where I taught. Not only that, but she also wanted to be the first to make a donation to the Andréa Rizzo Foundation.

As she placed her generous gift in my hand, she hugged me and said the words that resonated at my core. "Susan," she said intently, "you are turning the corner here. Think of the glass blower plunging raw glass into the fire, swirling it and melting it down until its glass-like state is no longer recognizable. The flames and the glassblower's artistry transform that molten mess into something exquisite and profoundly beautiful. God's grace is guiding you through the fire and an equally beautiful transformation is taking place within you as this glorious gift for children emerges," she said.

Sharon's words intensified my focus. I would silently repeat those words many times over.

As determined as I was, the question remained – what did I know about dance/movement therapy? I had no idea and I needed to find out fast. After thumbing through many of her New York University course textbooks, I found one written by a professor who Andréa had spoken of often. I picked up the phone and dialed information to get the phone number of NYU's dance department. I had prepared myself for a long search, but I was on the phone with Dr. Diane Duggan within minutes.

Compassionately, she shared with me her very recent remembrances of Andréa during their class sessions. "I remember her sensitivity and how bravely she expressed her own cancer experience through dance and movement during a presentation for the class. Such courage." She added wistfully, "I'll never forget those blonde curls."

I could envision my daughter in a dance studio at NYU, using dance to express her journey in a way that words could not.

Dr. Duggan explained that dance therapy was usually not practiced in local clinics. It was provided in both schools and hospitals.

"Hospitals?" Memorial Sloan-Kettering Cancer Center immediately popped into my head.

Andréa had always wanted to give back to the hospital that had saved her life, so my next call was to their pediatric department. This took a little more patience. I was transferred around the hospital switchboard from department to department until I felt dizzy and had left messages on more answering machines than I could begin to count. Each day, I'd attempt another round of calls, only to hear friendly voices that led me to more answering machines.

In the meantime, I studied Andréa's course binders and found that dance therapy was officially named dance/movement therapy and defined as the psychotherapeutic use of movement to further the emotional, cognitive, physical, and social integration of the individual. I still couldn't quite grasp the concept, but as I studied further, I found that dance/movement therapists are trained to access emotions like frustration, anger, anxiety, or fear. They help the child to express and release those emotions through movement and dance. In this way, the child finds new ways to cope and both an inner and physical healing takes place.

Armed with my rudimentary knowledge, I persisted in my pursuit through Memorial Sloan-Kettering's pediatric department until finally, one kind voice said, "You need to speak with the Administrator of Pediatrics."

Weeks later, my cell phone rang and there

on the other end of the line was Nina Pickett, the Administrator of Pediatrics herself. I went over my story with her and explained that we hoped to fund a pediatric dance therapy program through the memorial foundation we had set up in Andréa's name. Nina excitedly replied, "We offer music and art therapy, but not dance therapy. Truly, that is something I've always hoped we could offer our young patients. Write up your proposal and send it to me. Then we can talk."

That was it. This was the beginning of something that I could DO! Days later, I sat with Andréa's friends and colleagues in Terry Schimmel's sun-filled kitchen and prepared a mission statement. I knew nothing about mission statements either, but with everyone's help we pulled it together and were ready to put it in the mail to Nina.

I scheduled a meeting at the hospital and the following month my parents, brother, sister, their spouses, and Andréa's cousin, Chrissy, sat sipping coffee around a large mahogany table in a conference room at Memorial Sloan-Kettering Cancer Center. It had taken a lot of hand holding to get ourselves through that all too familiar lobby.

As we drank coffee and spread bagels with cream cheese, Nina Pickett took a deep breath and paused. She pulled out a sheaf of paper and her eyes welled with tears. "I found an email from Andréa sent to me just weeks before her death. She expressed her desire to volunteer at the hospital while she attended classes at NYU in the summer." The room fell silent. Nina continued, "Andréa explained that she had been treated and cured at Memorial Sloan-Kettering and wanted to give back in some way."

I gasped. Suddenly, I remembered the day Andréa had told me about having sent that email. She had been overflowing with excitement at the hope of being able to help. Now it seemed as if she were right there putting her stamp of approval on our mission.

After an hour and a half, we had a plan in place and felt ready to take on whatever was necessary to bring dance/movement therapy to the children at the hospital where Andréa had been cured. In my excitement I blurted out, "How about we call the program *Dréa's Dream*?" Everyone agreed it had an inviting ring to it and would draw children in.

It had been a difficult trip into the city that day, filled with trepidation, but we all left the hospital smiling with our hearts a little lighter. In my mind, I could envision the little dancing feet of children, experiencing movement in the same way that Andréa did – dancing to heal, to cope, and to express feelings that would lead to joy.

2003

My days had become full of phone calls and emails. In the midst of formulating ideas and learning about non-profits, I received a phone call from Janice DeFrances, the Principal of Narragansett Elementary School where Andréa had taught. I had come to know her as a friend and she continually amazed me with her caring and concern for my well being.

"Susan, we have to mark the upcoming anniversary of Andréa's death in a way that will bring beauty to this day and give you something to look forward to instead of the dread you must be feeling. Your family and their neighbors in Franklin Square have donated a piece of much-needed playground equipment and we'd like to hold the installation ceremony on that day." My eyes had welled with tears at the generosity that flowed all the way from the town that I'd grown up in on Long Island.

Janice went on, "Remember the sunflower seeds that Andréa's students were growing during her last week here with them?"

I stuttered a weak acknowledgement and fought hard not to cry.

Janice continued, "Once the students planted them outside of her classroom, those sunflowers grew to become enormous. The staff would like to expand that little patch into a full memorial garden outside of her classroom door."

Andréa had been part of the staff for only nine months. How could they still have such tenderness and compassion in their hearts for someone who they knew for such a short time?

"Do you remember the painting of the dancer with the flowing curls that our art teacher, Kathy Peabody, painted on the school wall outside of Andréa's classroom the day after her death?"

"Of course," I said quietly, thinking of the beautiful image of a dancer leaping into the air, long flowing curls trailing upward. I had been amazed by the immediate gesture of love offered by Kathy and even more stunned that the school allowed her to paint it to remain permanently on the brick wall.

"That dancer will be the focal point of the garden. We'll fill it with colorful perennials that will bloom during each part of the spring, summer, and fall. A local artist, Mimi Sammis, is designing a sculpture of three dancing children to serve as a constant reminder of the impact that Andréa had on our school. (Another gift from my family and their friends and neighbors.) All of this will be ready for a memorial service we'll hold at the garden on May 19th. Are you up for planting?"

My heart felt like it would burst with gratitude. My daughter was not being forgotten. She would live on in every bloom and I'd be right there beside those wonderful human beings who wanted to keep her memory alive.

On that glorious spring morning, my family accompanied me as I pulled my car into the same parking space Andréa had parked in each day. The parking lot was situated alongside a grassy slope and I could envision her bounding uphill, headed straight for her classroom door, anxious to start a new day. A small army of teachers and office staff, their family members in tow, unloaded mountains of fresh loam and crates of flowering plants while others had already cranked up a monstrous rototiller and were turning over the grass that lined the entire length of the building.

Janice DeFrances met me with a huge hug as Michaela and Michele, teachers who worked alongside Andréa with her special students, were shutting the tailgates of their trucks and shouting above the din to introduce me to their husbands. They were excited to show me the enormous rock they had dug up from Michele's yard. Shaped like a heart, they couldn't wait to plant it as a centerpiece in the middle of the garden. My friends, Barbara and Bill, held a rose bush and trellis, another gift for Andréa's garden. Andréa's cousins stood ready with packets of sunflower seeds to plant along the entire school wall. I glanced upward and thanked God for this outpouring of human kindness.

As we finished up many hours of digging and planting, gathering up shovels and trowels, I noticed Andréa's fellow teacher Chris pointing toward the May sky. It was a glorious blue, and the feathery clouds above us took our breath away when we figured out what Chris saw. I immediately ran to the car and grabbed the camera I brought along. I pointed it straight at the clouds that had formed themselves into a shape so similar to that of the dancer image painted on the school wall that it brought a loud gasp from the crowd looking skyward.

That ominous month of May was brightened by so many acts of kindness I couldn't have broken down if I tried. My fellow staff members at Memorial School had presented me with an enormous basket of children's books – each one based on a theme that had been a part of Andréa's life: dance, the beach, sunflowers. As I opened the cover of each colorful and beautifully illustrated book, I found Andréa's face smiling back at me. The teachers, with the help of my friend, Barbara Ulkus, had taken the time to design a bookplate with a photograph of Andréa and the name of the donor. There must have been over thirty books in the basket and as I read each one I was comforted in knowing that these books would sit on the shelves of the Memorial School library for years to come.

As I left the library with my class each week, invariably I'd hear one of my students pipe up, "Look, here's a picture of your daughter." Their excitement and smiles were gifts that quenched my thirst for reassurance that Andréa would live on in the hearts and minds of those who surrounded me.

May 19th arrived and the memorial service at Narragansett Elementary School brought family, friends, and colleagues together outside of Andréa's classroom. Facing the dancer on the wall we were surrounded by the garden, full of glorious flowering perennials and bordered with a colorful mixture of impatiens and marigolds that glistened under a sky full of sunshine. It was as beautiful as Janice had promised it would be. Stories of Andréa's loving ways were shared by her students. The children sang uplifting songs. Andréa's favorite book about a young dancer was read and shared. There was poetry, prayer, piano, mandolin, and flute music, and the dedication of a bronze sculpture bearing the words from a favorite quote: "Andréa Rizzo – One hundred years from now the world will be a better place because you made a difference in the life of a child."

Each year the luxurious garden expanded as the faithful crowd of gardeners picked the weekend closest to the anniversary of Andréa's death to be there with me – living proof that she was not forgotten.

Andréa had once said, "I live to dance." I kept that in my mind's eye as I planned each and every event that would support the Andréa Rizzo Foundation. As long as the Foundation thrived, Andréa and her love of dance would live on. For me, that seemed like a darn good reason to spend every minute of every day finding ways to grow this Foundation and Andréa's dream. I continued to be amazed at how all of the pieces needed for the Foundation's success seemed to come together, as if there was a force guiding all of us to the right people and places.

First, we searched for a New York based dance therapist. I turned to Sue Cohen, a friend of my two friends Rosanne and Michael. Sue was already a full-time dance therapist with Tomorrow's Children and offered lots of pointers about this profession that I still knew relatively little about. She suggested that I speak with Andréa's professor once again. After a long conversation, Dr. Diane Duggan said she had a few people in mind, but that one of them, Dr. Suzi Tortora, would be perfect as she had dedicated her life to working with children.

In the meantime, Memorial Sloan-Kettering had begun to advertise in search of the perfect person to fulfill Andréa's dream. One afternoon, as I sat munching on the last of my soggy salad while correcting homework during my twenty-five minute lunchtime at school, I received a call from Simone Zappa, Director of Integrative Medicines at the hospital. She updated me on the candidates who had been interviewed. She said that she had one more interview the next day and that this resumé stood out among the rest.

As promised, Simone called back the next day

and this time she sounded excited.

"We have found our dance therapist! The resumé was one thing, but the candidate offers so much more than we could have ever hoped for."

I listened as Simone read the list of the dance therapist's credentials and outstanding experience. Most of all, we were both impressed by her sensitivity to the needs of children with cancer. She had vividly described how dance and movement could transform their long days spent in hospital beds and facilitate their physical and emotional healing.

I asked Simone for her name. "Suzi," she said. This was the very same person that Diane Duggan had spoken so highly of! In that moment, I knew we were getting help from above to turn this dream into a reality.

Six months after we first set foot in that boardroom, *Dréa's Dream* pediatric dance therapy program was born. I thought back to our first meeting when Nina Pickett had told us that families are often too paralyzed by grief to take action quickly. I had accepted that as a personal challenge. I would do all that I could to make sure that dance and movement would find their way into every child's room on that pediatric floor.

Spring 2003

The day had come to see *Dréa's Dream* in action. Terry Schimmel, Katie Dugan, Paige Larrivee Boudreau (friends of Andréa's, among the many who were actively involved in the Foundation), drove with me to New Haven to catch the train into New York City. It was less than a year since Andréa had lost her life and we were filled with anticipation to see new life take shape in the form of *Dréa's Dream* at the very hospital where Andréa had been cured so many years ago.

Nina Pickett and Simone Zappa met us at the top of the escalator with open arms, embracing each of us with a warm and welcoming hug. I could feel my chest begin to tighten as we headed to the pediatric floor. I closed my eyes and envisioned Andréa as a small baby, sitting in one of the little red wagons that the hospital provides for parents to transport their children up and down the long halls and into the playroom. I fought to combat the emotion that began to consume me.

As we arrived on the fifth floor, the doors of the elevator opened and all friendly chatter fell silent as we stepped out. Even though I spent months here with my own child, it didn't make it easier to see the little, bald heads or the pale, thin bodies of children who were fighting for their lives. We solemnly and respectfully tried not to look at their sad, little faces.

Nina and Simone led us to that familiar playroom with sun pouring in through the large panes of painted glass. Suzi scurried to set up her music, scarves, various props, and instruments that would help to engage the patients in dance and movement. I thought back to the many hopeful talks I'd shared with Andréa when she'd envisioned the patients she would some day work with. She'd vividly described so many stimulating ways to distract them from their pain and get them up and out of bed – dancing.

I swallowed hard as a frail eight-year-old girl, Samantha, entered the room. Standing on one foot, she balanced herself by holding onto an IV pole – tubes and monitors everywhere. I quickly noticed that one pant leg was rolled up to cover the stump where her other leg had once been.

As soon as Samantha spotted Suzi, she broke into a smile that extended across her beautiful round face and suddenly the harsh reality of an amputated leg and bald head seemed to fall away. Samantha was ready to move.

Nina, Simone, Terry, Katie, and Paige all had tears ready to spill over or already streaming down their faces. I don't think that any of us expected that this was going to be so difficult to watch, yet so absolutely beautiful. I was struck by the emotion that Nina and Simone still felt freshly in their hearts, even after decades of working in a pediatric cancer ward. Their sensitivity and caring moved me beyond words.

Completely uninhibited as she steadied herself with the IV pole, Samantha asked for some rock music, "Britney Spears," she giggled. Suzi clicked on *Oops!... I Did It Again* and Samantha's face lit up. As the steady beat pounded from the iPod, she began hopping on her one foot. She wanted to see how many times she could jump. Laughing as she struggled to keep the beat, her energy seemed limitless – one, two, three…. when she got to ten, she yelled, "I'm still going!"

"Let's take a little break," Suzi suggested. "Here's a slower song by Britney and we'll just move our arms to this one." Suzi knew that Samantha might push herself too hard. Her enthusiasm and fearlessness were contagious and before we knew it we were all moving right along with her, making the same swaying motions with our arms, smiling through our tears, and letting her take the lead.

She had so little control over her needle-ridden life and if this moment offered her a chance to be calling the shots, then we were ready to follow. Samantha began to tire and Suzi chose a soothing song, asking her to lead us to her favorite place by using colorful scarves to describe it. She chose the beach and with diaphanous scarves flowing in front of her fragile body, she pretended to be jumping waves and then used her arms to assertively swim through each wall of blue. Her arms moved gracefully and found the rhythm and beat of the music easily. This was something she could do effortlessly, and it brought her to a comfortable and self-assured place in her mind as she leaned in and reached for each wave with complete confidence. By this time, we could all see Samantha's beach.

The music slowed to a gentle hush of soft sounds and Samantha reached forward with her arms and made a full circle as if holding a giant sun. She decided that it was time to lie down and sunbathe as Suzi assisted her in getting to the floor while the nurse on duty worked her magic to be sure that all tubes and needles would stay in place. As the soft and dreamy notes played on, Samantha took in the warm rays of the sun, her amputated leg the last thing on her mind. This was the perfect embodiment of Andréa's dream – a dance that ended in sunshine, with the hope for brighter days for children like Samantha.

Samantha's face and hopeful dance remained in the forefront of my thoughts as I sought the resources that I needed to bring dance/movement therapy to children who desperately needed it – those with cancer and special education needs. I gave another nod toward heaven and asked Andréa and God to be my guides.

Surprises seemed to pop up daily letting me know that I was proceeding along the right route. Early one morning, the phone rang and it was a national dance magazine editor asking for an interview about *Dréa's Dream* pediatric dance therapy program funded by the Andréa Rizzo Foundation. I was stunned at how fast word had spread, but with our website up and running, the internet would bring countless inquiries. Andréa's laptop, the only computer I had, quickly became a permanent fixture on my kitchen counter (our national headquarters) and I worked as fast as I could to keep up with the emails. I knew how important it was to get the word out about our work with pediatric cancer patients and children with special needs, but the thought of an interview with a national magazine made me nervous. I'd never been interviewed before. Thankfully, the journalist was patient and sincere in his interest to bring attention to our cause. I made it through, all the while wondering if I had included every last important detail.

Days after the interview, the phone rang and it was the art editor asking me if I had any photos of Andréa and *Dréa's Dream* in action. He sounded young, maybe in his early twenties. He paused and there was an extra long moment of silence. I wondered if something was wrong.

Then he said, "I knew Dréa. She taught at the after school program that I attended when I was a kid."

I caught my breath and couldn't respond as I remembered the after school job she held during her high school years.

He went on to tell me that he had graduated from college, moved to the next state and ended up working for a national magazine. What were the chances that he would be the one assigned do the layout for this article?

"I remember how much fun she was," he shared. Then he abruptly caught himself and asked if it was upsetting to me for him to talk about her.

"Upsetting me?" I asked incredulously. "There is no greater gift than sharing memories of Andréa with the people who knew her."

He went on, "She'd make each of us feel so special. She loved to play right along with us. She didn't act like a teacher. She acted like a friend. One day I fell off the swing and she was the first one at my side, giving me a huge hug and making sure I was okay. She even made me laugh. She didn't make a big deal because she understood that I was embarrassed. I'd always look forward to the days she worked. She'd just walk in and the whole room lit up. She had a way of making everything seem like fun."

We spoke for what seemed to be an hour. I just shook my head in disbelief at the coincidences that were piling up around the establishment of *Dréa's Dream*.

Summer 2003

Still knowing relatively little about fundraising, Andréa's friends took the lead and planned a walk-a-thon along the breathtakingly beautiful Cliff Walk in Newport, Rhode Island. We'd walk two miles, taking in the views overlooking Narragansett Bay – the same path Andréa had walked, rollerbladed, and ran along during her college years. It felt like the right thing to do in honor of her birthday. Salve Regina University had generously donated their recreation center for our starting line and ending point. Sunflowers would be tossed into the waters at the edge of the Cliff Walk. Balloons would be sent skyward, holding messages written on little sunflower papers. Dancers would perform. Friends and relatives would be by my side to get me through a day that held both dread and hope.

Months of preparation led to the event – days spent filling out forms, gathering items to fill baskets that would be raffled, buttons ordered for each walker to wear bearing Andréa's smiling face with a little reminder: "Love life; keep her dream dancing on." Bushels full of sunflowers were donated for us to carry along the way.

August 15th finally arrived and as always, I automatically awoke at 7:15 a.m. – the moment of Andréa's birth. I had always chuckled about this in the past, but this once magical coincidence now brought pain. How would I get through the day without her there to hug and share in the opening of the many gifts that would have been on her birthday "wish list?"

As I tentatively rose from bed, I smiled to see the sunshine. Since her death the shining of the sun had evoked only bitterness – for how could it shine without Andréa here? But today, we needed the sun's blessing on all those who walked in her memory.

My family had arrived from New York twenty-four hours earlier and now lie sleeping after a night filled with placing the finishing touches on signs, raffle posters, and photo collages. I couldn't have faced this morning without them. I pushed myself out of Andréa's bed and proceeded to the shower. The hot water both soothed me and awakened my hopes for a day that would honor my child. I pulled on my sunflower yellow Andréa Rizzo Foundation t-shirt and tugged my ponytail through the sunflower adorned baseball cap that a friend had sent me. My sister-in-law, Marilou, had found flip-flops with big sunflowers sitting on top. They smiled up at me and I felt strength begin to rush in.

I said a little prayer as I wished Andréa a 'Happy Birthday' and walked downstairs while my family helped me to load up my Jeep and embark on what would be the first of many fundraising adventures.

As the troupe of volunteers frantically set up the decorations, tables, chairs, posters, and a myriad of other things that transformed the expansive porch and slate patio that spread out in front of Rodgers Recreation Center, one of the young dancers who would perform that day approached me with tears in her eyes. She shyly looked at me through a moppet of red hair, her voice quivering as she began to speak. She explained that she had loved to dance since she was very young. When she heard of Andréa's dream, she'd made Andréa's dream her own. She too wanted to become a dance/movement therapist. We hugged each other and I felt the energy that would multiply and carry me through the days ahead. I was stunned to discover that this mission would also impact young dancers who wanted to combine their love of dance with compassion in the same way that Andréa did. I never imagined that this youthful exuberance would become a part of my new life.

The crowd began to arrive. Among them were my faithful friends and family, Andréa's college friends, their parents, her former professors, dancers, dance therapists, friends of friends, and perfect strangers who had seen our flyers tacked up on scores of bulletin boards around town. Blue t-shirts emblazoned with the Foundation's newly crafted logo stood out and the yellow and blue balloons produced a flurry of Andréa's favorite colors. Everyone pitched in to help. Even Andréa's youngest cousins, Justin and Makenzi – only six and seven at the time – excitedly set up their own table and cash box. They were anxious to be in charge of soda and water sales for the day.

I'd prepared a speech to express my gratitude. How would I get through it? Public speaking was not my forté. What if I began to cry? My voice quivered through the many pages I'd written as I tried to maneuver through the flipping of the papers while holding a microphone. I made it to the end and then breathed a sigh of relief, hoping I'd adequately thanked each and every one who had helped make this day possible. Dancers from all over New England had come to volunteer their talent and perform for the crowd of nearly two hundred. I could see Andréa dancing with every hip swing and kick.

Before taking off on our walk, there was one special guest to introduce. Jonathan Walker, a nine-year-old patient from Memorial Sloan-Kettering Cancer Center, had arrived with his parents and brother. The crowd fell silent as they listened to the impact *Dréa's Dream* had on his cancer experience. Jonathan's family explained how the dance therapist had him up out of his bed on days when they couldn't get him to lift his head. They told of techniques they had learned to help him use movement as a way to calm his anxiety about upcoming treatments – sliding his feet, swaying to energizing music, and swirling streamers to a steady beat. All the while, Jonathan stood with the help of a brace, smiling from ear to ear – happy to have the chance to say thank you. As he grasped the microphone his soft voice touched the hearts of the crowd, "Dancing made my days so much happier. Thank you so much." I could hear the sniffles around me and saw tears in many eyes.

As the walk began, the breeze off of Narragansett Bay kept everyone cool. I looked out at the crowd ahead of me, in awe that they had taken the time to be there to honor Andréa's life and support her dream. With a definite upbeat feeling in the air, we rounded the last bend and approached the arch leading up to Rodgers Recreation Center. The DJ's music blared and for the first time I was able to listen – not wanting to run and hide from familiar refrains.

Andréa's team of friends had run ahead to greet the returning crowd, and I hugged each of them while they passed out baked goods and fed the hungry walkers. Their presence in my life and willingness to work together to keep Andréa's memory alive kept me afloat.

As the last group of dancers performed for our finale, I embraced more people than I could count. I had to let them know how important their support was to me. They were my lifeline.

After a day filled with a mix of tears, joy, sadness, and overwhelming gratitude, I found a letter waiting for me in my mailbox when I arrived back home. Dragging in the last of the decorations, props, and fundraising signs that would crowd my tiny condo for years to come, I saw that the return address on the envelope was from Dr. Suzi Tortora. Collapsing into the couch between boxes of leftover t-shirts, I read her words.

Dear Susan and Foundation Members,

Each day at Memorial Sloan-Kettering Cancer Center I am filled with awe at the children, the families, the staff. The love and care and kindness in and of itself creates such an atmosphere of healing. I feel embraced. Everyone has welcomed my presence and the gift of dance therapy from the Andréa Rizzo Foundation.

My memories already are full – of the little Austrian girl who took me on a journey to the sun, the sky, and the flowers through our dance, despite the language barrier. And the 2 ½ year old who stood up on his bed and jumped and twirled and swayed with me, stepping and leaping over the tubes he was attached to sustaining our dancing journey for twenty minutes.

Then there was the nine-year-old who adjusted her

dancing style to each change of music, portraying a Spanish dancer, a tango partner, and a peppy teenager, culminating her dance in a soft, warm embrace to herself – seeming to say in her silent gestures, that everything will be okay. She had just lost her leg to cancer the week before.

Lastly, there was the teen, studying to be a professional dancer, who stood up and performed a dancer's warm up with me and quietly allowed her tears to softly roll down her cheeks as her body remembered those moves that she hadn't felt in eighteen months.

As my work begins here at Memorial Sloan-Kettering Cancer Center, it is I who must thank all of you.

Sincerely,
Suzi

I folded up the letter, held it tightly as I walked upstairs to my bedroom, tucked it under my pillow, and said a prayer to Andréa. We would remain a team.

October 2003

As autumn arrived, my entire family was in the throes of planning yet another golf outing on Long Island. It would become an annual event to support Dréa's Dream and representatives from Memorial Sloan-Kettering attended to show their appreciation. I gazed in surprise as raffle ticket tables had been organized and a vast breakfast and luncheon was prepared while everyone ambitiously set about their tasks. I arrived the night before and was stunned to see my entire family hard at work. Once again, tremendous generosity and effort poured forth from my family's friends on Long Island, and over one hundred golfers became our faithful supporters. How would I ever be able to let each of them know how much this meant to me?

With another school year in full swing, thoughts of Andréa's students and concern over their well-being lingered in my mind. I worried about the impact that the loss of a beloved teacher had on their fragile lives. Many of them were severely disabled and it must have been hard for them to understand why she left them so suddenly. My sister, Jill, thought of a generous way to keep Andréa's caring spirit alive for her students. On Thanksgiving, my nieces and nephews wrapped toys my family purchased from the Christmas wish lists of Andréa's most needy students. As Jami, Erika, Gary Jr., Tayler, Justin, and Makenzi took turns cutting, wrapping, and taping the mountain of boxes, they became Santa's elves for a child who was close to their cousin's heart. We thought of one child in particular who Andréa had spoken of often. I contacted his single mom and we set a date for the holiday delivery.

In the dusk of a late November afternoon, after a long day of teaching in Connecticut, I drove through a small Rhode Island town following country roads that meandered past dilapidated farmhouses. I circled through a few dead ends before I found the mailbox bearing the number I was looking for. I maneuvered my Jeep up the steep dirt driveway leading to the small, wooden frame home of Matthew, a child with cerebral palsy and confined to a wheelchair – unable to walk or to speak.

Carrying large bags overflowing with gifts, I hobbled up the lopsided steps to the front door, with its peeling paint and broken hinge. I heard a voice from inside the house, "Door's open. Come on in!"

Walking through the door, Matthew's mother, no more than twenty-five, greeted me warmly. I glanced ahead into the living room and caught sight of Matthew. I tried to hide my alarmed reaction. There he sat, slumped over, weighed down by his little head that couldn't remain upright no matter how hard he tried. He was attached to a breathing apparatus, a tracheotomy scar visible on his limp neck. His eyes strained to look up at me, but he couldn't lift his head to make eye contact. I bent down and met his gaze, letting him know who I was and why I had come. He stared at me with big brown eyes that told of the frustration born of his inability to speak.

Andréa had spoken often of Matthew and her visits to the hospital to see him during stretches of time when he was unable to attend school. She'd told me of the nurse who accompanied him during class, adjusting his feeding tube, and how his grandmother visited the classroom and advocated for her sorrowfully helpless, but very precious, little grandson. Andréa had learned so much by working with the nurse, the grandmother, and the many therapists who accompanied him each day.

I sat down next to him on a threadbare couch and wondered what Andréa would do to make him smile and catch his wandering gaze. As soon as he saw the gifts, his excitement began to erupt, with arms waving and the best laughing sounds he could muster. His stiff little hands glided over the holiday paper and I helped him to unwrap the gifts, with me doing most of the unwrapping. We opened just a few and his mother placed the remainder of the presents under the Christmas tree.

I reached into my pocket and took out a photo of Andréa with her arms wrapped around Matthew. Whether he recognized her or not didn't matter. We had brightened one of her student's lives and that was all that she would have wanted.

Escaping 2003

With the holidays weighing down on me once again, I had prepared for my next "Get Away From Christmas" and was on my way to Barbados in time to escape the anxiety-ridden days leading up to December 25th. On Christmas morning I woke up on an ocean liner for the second year in a row. I immediately noticed the gray skies and ominous clouds that hovered over the ship. I grabbed a hooded sweatshirt and brought my bag of books with me and headed for the quietest spot I could find in the most remote corner of the top deck. I had learned the previous year that Christmas songs were the perpetual background music for a holiday cruise. My friend Jean prepared me with the gift of a headset and CD player stocked with classical music to block out the taunting refrains of *Jingle Bells* and *Joy to the World*. As the day wore on, I sat in a gray mist, headset tightly secured, consumed by a stack of "self-help" books for managing a grief-stricken soul, and writing in my journal in hopes of finding the right words to add to my own book – the one that Andréa and I had pledged to finish. I squinted up at the sky and saw the sun breaking through the thick clouds. Not thinking too much of it, I got back to my reading and writing. Looking up again, I did a double take. Arching from one side of the ship's bow to the other was a glorious rainbow. There had been no other rainbow during the trip except this one on Christmas Day. I had to believe this was yet another Christmas gift from Andréa.

When spring break came, I once again sought the healing balm of warmth, sunshine, and salt air. This time I boarded a plane in Hartford, bound for Mexico. I'd decided that cruise ships were too full of happy families and gaiety. I arrived alone on Isla Mujeres after a half-hour ferry ride from Cancun. This quiet island had just the right combination of American tourists and friendly Mexicans to make me feel relaxed. I wasn't feeling the pangs of loneliness that brought on the attacks of anxiety. Sitting on a white sand beach just outside the Hotel Cabanas De Maria, I sipped my morning pineapple juice and nibbled on a simple wedge of bread – the complimentary breakfast of the day. I knew a single, middle-aged woman must have appeared out of place to passersby. I'd developed a morning ritual on each of my trips alone. I'd get out my now tattered journal and pages of notes and begin to write. This was my way of getting up to face a day of searching – for what I wasn't quite sure.

A spry older woman, maybe in her late sixties, approached me with a friendly, "Hello." She looked like an American enjoying a vacation. I could see her curiosity was piqued as she spied the papers sprawled out on my lap and she asked what I was doing. My being alone coupled with the paperwork and the intensity with which I was writing made me stick out from the others who were sunbathing and relaxing in the sand. I shrugged my shoulders and offhandedly told her I was writing a book.

"A book? About what?" she asked.

"Oh, just a story," I replied vaguely. I wondered why people feel so free to ask such personal questions of perfect strangers, but I'd learned to dodge them. Who wanted to hear my sad explanation, really? We chatted for a few minutes and as she left she must have been imagining an exciting mystery with perhaps some adventure thrown in.

With my concentration broken, I looked out at the sea. A sailboat sat anchored several hundred feet offshore, rocking in the gentle turquoise waters of the Caribbean. The morning sun created a sea of radiant crystals. I saw the city of Cancun in the distance, confirming my good choice to stay on this tiny, peaceful island with its colorful Mexican culture and warm, friendly people. I let the calm wash over me.

I wondered if a new life on a tropical island would be less painful. Would new people, places, and things be the cure? There would be no daily reminders – only memories that I kept sacredly to myself. When home, I ached as the change of seasons opened my wounds with each turning leaf, each snowflake, and each blossoming flower reminding me that time kept passing and Andréa wasn't with me.

It felt disrespectful of my past to continue walking in my old shoes, driving the same car on the same roads, and exposing myself to the sights and reminders of a life that no longer existed. Remaining in the same place was like rubbing salt in my wounds and I wondered if a new place, one so completely different from what I had known would help to ease my pain and clear my vision for a bearable future.

But with each phone call from caring supporters, every hug I received from my students and colleagues, each thoughtful note that stood on my nightstand (powerful reminders of the love that surrounded me), and all the hours spent talking about shared memories of Andréa with friends and family, I grew to understand that their emotional and physical support was crucial for my survival – so I stayed.

2004

Sitting in a small office, stacked with boxes of surgical masks, rubber gloves, and paper gowns, the antiseptic smell of Memorial Sloan-Kettering Cancer Center hung in the air. Andréa's college friend Katie Dugan, now a Board Member, Jill, my mother and I had just finished an afternoon of meetings with administrators discussing plans to expand *Dréa's Dream* pediatric dance therapy program. What they once thought would be a three-hour-a-week program was turning into a twenty-hour-per-week program because of the results the medical staff were observing in the patients who received dance/movement therapy.

We were on the edge of our seats as we anxiously waited to view video footage of the multisensory dance/movement therapy technique that Dr. Suzi Tortora had begun to develop for children receiving the painful 3f8 treatment for neuroblastoma. The drugs caused muscle spasms and Suzi had become an integral part of the medical team during these treatments.

We watched intently as the treatment of a very sick baby began. At eighteen months old the child was the same age Andréa had been when diagnosed with neuroblastoma. I immediately identified with the young mother as she held her screaming child. Inconsolable, the baby whimpered in pain while Suzi calmed her as she dimmed the lights and played soft music while moving the child's hands and then her feet in rhythm with the music. Suzi took cues from the baby's reaction and knew which movements would bring the results she was hoping for. Amid the tubes attached to the baby's arms there was one that connected to a heart monitor. We watched as her heart rate slowed and she became enthralled with the movement. Within a few minutes the baby stopped crying. By engaging her other senses, Suzi was able to distract the baby from the pain sensation. Suzi proceeded to sway with the baby and move her tiny feet back and forth. The movement, even if just a simple foot movement, seemed to catch the child's attention and give her something to focus on.

In another clip, a young boy, about nine or ten, danced near his hospital bed. After three months in the hospital, his white blood cell count improved enough for him to move to the Ronald McDonald House down the street. He held hands with Suzi and they did a few slow turns together in the space beside his bed. The music was soothing and Suzi asked him how he was feeling about leaving the hospital that had been his home for many months. He quickly stepped up the beat of his dance as he and Suzi did a few twirls. He seemed so engrossed in their movements. I was astonished as I watched the expression on this young boy's face change as he danced. His conflicted feelings, so clearly visible at first, gradually emerged as proud and confident. By the time the dance ended, he had worked through his confusion: happy to leave the hospital but fearful to re-enter the world – bald and frail.

Curious about this sensitive boy I asked, "Where is he from?"

"Wakefield, Rhode Island," Simone replied.

"That's the town next to where I live," I said with complete surprise.

When I returned home, I found that Terry Schimmel knew his family as her husband worked with the boy's father and they lived right down the street from her. When the family became aware of the coincidence, we all became fast friends.

That same day, we had a chance to sit in on a bedside session. Three-year-old Sarah couldn't leave her room for lack of strength and a compromised immune system. She sat in her hospital bed with the covers tucked up under her chin, her mouth drawn into a sad pout. We had to gown-up and put on surgical masks before entering her room.

When Suzi arrived, Sarah's young dad, Jason, laughed as he described how Sarah had been asking for the "dancing lady." Wearing his Boston Red Sox cap, Jason carefully lifted his daughter into his arms and waltzed with her to the soothing beat. His love and affection toward his little girl was obvious. He assisted her as she tried to stand and bounce to the rhythmic music now blaring from the speakers of the iPod. Holding onto the side of her bed, feet now on the floor, Sarah couldn't resist the thumping beat of the peppy music. Suzi stood alongside her and mimicked Sarah's movements, allowing her to be the leader and choreograph her own simple childlike dance. Sarah laughed at Suzi's motions and before we knew it she'd let go of the bed and let the rhythm take over, hands in the air, swaying in delight. I knew that this seemingly silly little dance had done wonders for Sarah both physically and mentally. Her dad stood watching with tears in his eyes.

Months after our hospital visit, Katie attended a holiday party in Boston with friends from work. In walked a little girl dressed in red velvet and a big red bow on top of her bald little head – the cruel and obvious sign of cancer. Katie did a double take. She leaned in and whispered to the hostess, "Where is she being treated?"

"Memorial Sloan-Kettering Cancer Center," the hostess quietly replied.

Katie gasped. "Is her name Sarah?"

"Yes." Pointing unobtrusively she added, "Those are her parents, Michele and Jason. They are my cousins." Katie immediately made the connection. This was the same little girl we had observed dancing with her dad at Memorial Sloan-Kettering Cancer

Center hundreds of miles away.

These kinds of coincidences became part of the miracle of *Dréa's Dream*. I'd just look up at heaven and thank Andréa for letting me know that she was doing her part.

Lessons I Learned

- When your heart has a hole in it, keep it open to the gifts that surround you – no matter how small. You will be amazed at how your heart fills with gratitude. A saving grace.

- Devote yourself to helping others. It will give you a positive focus and keep you busy.

- Take your child's passion and give it to the world. If you create a memorial for your child, be sure to include their name in the title. It will bring you comfort each time you say it, a way to cherish and honor the life that you lost.

- While planning a memorial, hold meetings at your home with friends and family. This will be your first steps toward "entertaining" again – but with a safe framework. The focus will be on your child and positive plans (not sad and grief-filled plans).

- Brainstorm with friends who are willing and excited to share their ideas for your new endeavor. It's the beginning of a new and uncharted stage of your life and you will need their support.

- Magical moments will occur. Things will fall into place and happenings will seem heaven sent. Be prepared to be surprised. Just remain open to the gifts.

- Reach out to other families who have created memorials for loved ones. They will be happy to share what they have learned and you both will find comfort in knowing that you are not alone.

Gotta' Dance

"Dancing has always been a big part of my life. I began dancing when I was three years old and I can't imagine ever stopping. Dancing for me, is an escape, a stress reliever and seems to put everything into perspective. It makes me feel free. I live to dance. I've gotta' dance!"

Andréa Rizzo

Lesson 7

Reverencé : a bow in which one foot is pointed in front and the body leans forward

"Life is not about waiting for the storms to pass... It's about learning how to dance in the rain."

~ Vivian Greene

November 2007

Letters from young patients as well as dancers flooded my mailbox. Filled with heartwarming stories of how their lives had been touched by *Dréa's Dream*, they also expressed a desire to help. One letter in particular assured me we were doing important work and would transform the lives of children with cancer:

To the Andréa Rizzo Foundation,

I'm 17 years old and I am so thankful to the Andréa Rizzo Foundation for the wonderful support I received through their dance therapy program as a patient at Memorial Sloan-Kettering Cancer Center this past year. I was diagnosed in December 2006, at age 16, with a rare sarcoma of the liver. After undergoing major surgery, I was treated with chemotherapy from January until June 2007. The protocol was extremely aggressive and intense and much of the time I felt very sick, both from the surgery and the side effects of the drugs.

Although I've danced all of my life, I really didn't know much about dance therapy, but one day, during one of my early in-patient stays, the dance therapy team of Suzi Tortora, Ed.D. and Jocelyn Shaw, showed up in my hospital room. Suzi and Jocelyn were so friendly and warm that I felt a bond with them right away. I wasn't feeling at all energetic, but their enthusiasm was contagious, and within moments of their arrival, I got up out of bed, which was no easy task, and participated in my first dance therapy session.

My mom, who is not a dancer, was invited to participate and joined us. We went around in a circle and everyone contributed some movements to express how they were feeling. During that one session, we danced through our anxiety, fear, and anger and were able to find a relaxed state for both mind and body. It was so much fun and such a release.

From that day on, I always looked forward to Suzi or Jocelyn coming to dance with me. Any family member who was with me was always invited to participate and boy, you haven't lived until you've seen my father do dance therapy. These therapists were able to interact with him without laughing which is more than I could say for myself. They are truly amazing!

Even when I couldn't get out of bed, they were able to transport my thoughts out of the hospital, into the sky, the ocean, a sandy beach, wherever my fancy would take me that day. We used some of my favorite songs to break out of that room and soar. I was able to find a calm place to be after their visits and that state would stay with me for a long time.

Dance therapy made all the difference in getting through my treatment in good spirits, which was so important. I believe that even though this illness happened to me, my life has been greatly enriched by meeting these wonderful, caring, talented dance therapists.

Please do all you can to enable other young people to benefit from this program the way that I did. It has honestly changed my life.

Thank you very much.
Julie

I felt I had to do more to make the Foundation grow. I wanted to expand *Dréa's Dream* pediatric dance therapy program to other hospitals and schools across the country.

I could have used another ten hours in each day. I awoke before dawn, allowing time before my teaching day to catch up on thank you notes to supporters and email correspondence that flooded my inbox overnight. I became an expert at writing newsletters, press releases, brochures, and flyers. Graphic design became part of my repertoire and logos and dance icons filled my dreams. During my hour-long commute home from teaching, I'd use my phone's headset and converse with corporate executives, newspaper reporters, hospital and school administrators, and young dancers – all interested in the work we were doing and requesting more information. I'd continue my conversations while making my daily stop at the post office, phone now propped on my shoulder, as I filled boxes full of promotional materials to be sent nationwide. Once home, I'd hop out of the car, still finishing up my calls and I would reach for the laptop as I stepped inside the door of my condo. I'd plunge into the countless hours of follow-up needed for each of the calls and then I'd attack one project or another that sat waiting for me from the night before – usually, a grant application. By 1:00 a.m., I'd call it quits, my mind still racing with new ideas while I tossed in bed trying to catch a few hours of sleep before getting up and repeating this routine all over again.

"We have to figure out a way to get national attention for the Foundation on television," Terry Schimmel, now a Board Member, announced as we were wrapping up one of our late-night board meetings.

"What shows?" I asked, since I still didn't watch TV.

"I can think of lots of them," a perky voice chimed in from the back of the room. We'd been lucky enough to find a young, energetic, and bright work-study student who was full of great ideas and she attended all of our meetings. Sarah Puerini became our breath of fresh air and my right hand. Excitedly she began rattling off all of the shows she could think of within a millisecond. "How about *Oprah, Ellen DeGeneres, Dancing With the Stars,* or *So You Think You Can Dance*?" I forced a smile, but felt my shoulders slump. I couldn't imagine how we would begin to accomplish that lofty goal.

Dutifully but half-heartedly, I put together all of the brochures and letters of testimony about *Dréa's Dream* we had collected from hospitals and schools, and sent packets upon packets of information about our cause to popular dance-related TV shows. It was a shot in the dark.

One night, an email popped up on my computer in the midst of a planning meeting for an upcoming fundraiser. I got goose bumps as I read it aloud. Kindness and compassion seemed to shoot through cyberspace from the other side of the country. An assistant at *Dancing With the Stars* was touched by the information I had sent to her. She offered me tickets to the show as a raffle or auction item to support our cause. This was an enormous gift and I wanted to share it in a special way. Immediately, I thought of Julie and the letter she had written to us after her experience at Memorial Sloan-Kettering Cancer Center. With her love of dance, I knew she would be thrilled to attend *Dancing With the Stars*.

I sent back an email to the assistant asking if we could make arrangements to escort a lovely young patient named Julie and her mom, Stacey, to the show, rather than using the tickets to help raise funds. We couldn't pass up the opportunity to brighten a cancer patient's life. She excitedly helped me make the plan a reality. Our only dilemma was that we would somehow have to come up with the airfare to get Julie and Stacey from New York to Los Angeles.

Determined to find a solution, Katie scanned the roster of dancers for that season. Actress and artist Jane Seymour would be dancing on the show. Katie telephoned Jane's art gallery in Los Angeles and spoke with Susan Nagy Luks, the art director at Jane's Coral Canyon Publishing. Taking the time to listen, Susan promised she would speak with Jane about our mission. Within twenty-four hours, Susan called Katie to say that Jane was touched by our story and wanted to donate one of her original *Open Hearts* paintings for us to auction and hopefully cover the cost of the airfare. Susan picked out the artwork, readied it for shipping, and had it sent out the next day.

We planned an auction in Newport, Rhode Island, and raised the money to cover the airfare for both mother and daughter. On a late autumn day, Julie and Stacey took off from New York, bound for Los Angeles while I boarded a plane in Providence.

I met them at their hotel nearby the studio. Julie radiated warmth, sincerity, and genuine gratitude. Her big smile exuded a healthy presence, although I knew she had just been through a surgery so serious that many would not have survived.

We'd been instructed by the audience coordinator to get to West Hollywood early to meet our personal ABC representative at the studio door. As soon as he spotted us, we were immediately directed to the VIP line, quickly guiding us right through security. The ballroom was every bit the epitome of Hollywood. The enormous mirror ball sparkled like the crown jewels. Rows of red velour seats encircled the dance floor. Glitz, glitter, and glamour were everywhere.

Practically dancing ourselves, we followed our representative as he ushered us forward and downward toward the dance floor. VIP, it turned out, meant front row! I kept my eyes on Julie's face – full of excitement and wonder. She glowed with anticipation. Tears welled up in my eyes. I wanted to hug her and remember this moment forever.

We let out a collective gasp when we found our names taped to the seats directly next to the judges' stand! The audience coordinator at *Dancing With the Stars* had arranged for our special seating and now ran out to greet us with open arms.

By now my heart was pounding. I gushed words of gratitude and couldn't hold back the tears when the costume designer personally delivered a special bracelet for Julie. It matched the ones the dancers would be wearing that night. ABC Eyewitness News had been tipped off about Julie being a special guest and there were reporters waiting in the wings to speak with her. A photo shoot after the show with all of the dancers on the dance floor would top off this over-the-top evening.

Spotlights shone at our feet and our faces were flushed from the radiant heat, but also from the sheer excitement that we felt in every cell of our bodies as we sat there taking in every thrilling detail of this unforgettable night. I wished I could somehow give a group hug to all of the people who had made this happen for Julie.

As the show got underway, she was out of her seat with excitement, bouncing, and cheering for all of the dancers. During a commercial break, her enthusiasm caught the eye of the audience interviewer. He asked her how she had gotten her tickets to the show. As she spoke into his microphone, she told her story and the ballroom fell into a quiet hush of compassion. This caught the attention of *Dancing With the Stars* judge Carrie Ann Inaba. During the next commercial break, Carrie Ann came over to our seats to say hello to our exuberant patient. Julie told her about the Andréa Rizzo Foundation. While jotting down the Foundation's contact information, Carrie Ann explained that she understood the healing capacity of dance as well as the mind, body, and spirit connection that occurs within dance/movement therapy. She promised to get back to me. She later became the Andréa Rizzo Foundation's National Spokesperson, helping to raise funds to support our mission and to kick off *Dréa's Dream* at Children's Hospital Los Angeles and Mattel Children's Hospital UCLA. She brightened so many patient's lives for us.

That very night, after the VIP treatment and ABC photo shoots, I sped away in a cab that was waiting outside the studio and jumped on the red-eye back to Hartford. With dark circles under my eyes and adrenaline still pumping, I arrived home just in time to greet my second grade students at 8:25 a.m., Eastern Standard Time.

My colleagues waited at my classroom door anxious to hear every detail of my trip to Hollywood. They had watched the show the night before and saw me sitting there alongside Julie. I'd been wearing a bright pink scarf so they wouldn't miss us. These dear friends looked forward to every one of the gifts that flowed toward *Dréa's Dream,* right along with me. They had been there to share each and every piece of my old life and now were part of my new life providing me with love and support every step of the way.

The excitement of my glamorous excursion had washed over some of the pain that filled my heart. I was grateful for this gift – like a colorful parachute drifting with me in tow, taking me in a new direction.

Daily, the consistency of being with my students calmed my heart. Each day began with their smiles and hugs and filled my need for "unconditional love." I'd beam inside as I watched them wobble into the classroom with proud, toothless grins under the weight of their huge backpacks. I wondered how they had made it down two long hallways from the front lobby, while carrying what appeared to be thirty-pound loads on their little backs. As they unloaded their oversized sacks with homework, pretzels, and pencils pouring onto the floor in front of their cubbies, I hoped their parents had kissed them each morning and that they were cherished at home. I'd be reminded of the days long ago when Andréa would wake each morning and together we got ready for school.

Friends wondered how I had gone back to work in the school where Andréa and I had shared so many memories. But these beautiful children brought me back to my happiest days. Unknowingly, they brightened my broken life and reignited that spark of maternal love. They didn't know they made me smile inside and kept my heart full.

Each day began the same way: the bell rang, the Pledge of Allegiance was said, and my classroom was up and running, offering me new strength within a familiar and energizing routine. I thrived on this routine.

December 2007

My criteria for a Christmas getaway had narrowed to the most remote spots where I would be sure to find protection from the holiday lights, music, and festivities. I found it on Tortola in the British Virgin Islands. A quiet resort boasted the most beautiful, serene stretch of white sand and turquoise water. At the bottom of a winding hill, full of hairpin turns, there wasn't much to offer vacationers except a few villas and an exquisite beach –perfect for me.

As usual on Christmas day, I got up early to be sure I'd see the rainbow that I had now come to expect. Packing up my camera and very faded journal, I headed for the beach.

Impatiently, I tried to get the key out of the lock to my villa's door, but it wouldn't release. Finally, with no time to spare, I just left it hanging there and ran down to the beach for fear I'd miss any glimpse of a rainbow.

Standing along the shore I found a couple looking upward at the remains of what I overheard them say was "a stunning rainbow."

"A rainbow?" I asked apprehensively.

"Oh, yes. It was brilliant."

Crestfallen, I retreated to a corner of the beach, hidden by a rocky cliff. I had missed my gift from Andréa. As tears fell, I bowed my head and prayed. "I am so sorry, Dréa. Please forgive me. Please dear God, please give me another chance," I whispered.

Several minutes later I lifted my head to see a rainbow forming off to my left. Then, a second dazzling rainbow appeared on my right. The two crisscrossed in the blue sky over the glistening water. Beyond a doubt, this was my Christmas gift from Andréa.

Ancient sayings suggest that rainbows are the bridge between heaven and earth. The rainbow painting hanging on the wall in my home was a work of art that Andréa had painted with watercolors at seven years old. The beautifully printed program we had prepared for her funeral service was on a background print of clouds with her photo in a rainbow up in the left-hand corner. A poem entitled *Togetherness* was printed on the same rainbow paper, and I had given it as gifts to friends and family in those first few months after her death. One remained tucked in the sun visor of my car – just as a reminder. A Christmas rainbow was a perfectly appropriate gift.

January 2008

Working around the clock on the growth and success of the Foundation became a full-time job. There really weren't enough hours in each day, but I continued to teach and found the energy I needed through meeting new people and sharing ideas for the Foundation's growth. It became my source of fuel – moving me onward. When a donation came in the mail, there always seemed to be a special story attached to it bringing tears to my eyes. A widower from Indiana wrote of his wife who loved to dance and had taught elementary school for many years. He had found our Foundation while searching for a dance-related charity. He felt it would make her happy to know that children could be helped through the gift of dance therapy. Her colleagues also made a donation and included heartfelt notes about their friend.

Young children donated their birthday gifts

to help *Dréa's Dream*. A check for $700 appeared in my mailbox from a girl who held a dance fundraiser for her Confirmation Service Project. One very young dancer asked each friend to bring a brand new teddy bear instead of a birthday gift to her party so the bears could be donated to the children at the Ronald McDonald House in New York City where we now held dance therapy sessions. One girl centered her Bat Mitzvah project around *Dréa's Dream* and gave over $3,000 to our cause. Another donated the ballet slippers that had been part of the centerpieces at her special event, hoping that the young patients would enjoy a new pair of dance shoes.

I cried when I opened an invitation to a Sweet Sixteen party for a dancer, Danielle Hernandez, from New Jersey. She had dedicated her special celebration to our cause. The handmade invitations explained that each guest could make a donation of $16 and all of these gifts would be given to help the Andréa Rizzo Foundation.

Each day there were new gifts. A college graduate, Jennifer Whitley, contacted me to say that she was interested in the field of dance therapy. She wanted to produce a full-scale fundraising event in New York City. Before I knew it she had rallied a group of ambitious and compassionate young professionals and they began what would become an annual dance exhibition and reception. "How does 'Heart & Feet' sound?" Jennifer bubbled with excitement as she had come up with the clever name for the event. I loved it!

As people reached out to help, healing occurred for me as well as for some of them – and, of course, our patients. When eight-year-old Brandon Audet from New Jersey was diagnosed with a rare form of thyroid cancer, his eleven-year-old sister, Ashley felt distraught. She stood in the hall outside of her brother's hospital room and cried for him and for all of the other children as they received painful and debilitating treatments. She wondered what she could do to help them.

During those long hours spent waiting for Brandon's treatment to be completed, Brandon's mother, Lynn, sat tensely at his bedside, trying to find a distraction. She casually picked up a *Woman's Day* magazine and flipped through the pages. Although her mind was elsewhere, an article about the Andréa Rizzo Foundation caught her eye and spoke to her heart. Her spirits soared as she read of Andréa's complete recovery. There was hope for her son, Lynn thought.

At the end of the *Woman's Day* article, she read that dancers were helping the Andréa Rizzo Foundation to spread *Dréa's Dream* pediatric dance therapy program to hospitals and schools by holding benefit performances and dance-a-thons. Ashley had danced since she was three; dance was the love of her life. Lynn looked up and saw Ashley's blank stare and understood she felt helpless as Brandon lay in his hospital bed. She made an instant connection, one of those aha moments that felt completely right.

Lynn sat down next to Ashley and after reading the article together, they looked at each other with hope in their eyes. Ashley knew how good dance made her feel, and she understood that dance therapy could help the children around her to feel good, too. They immediately began planning how they could contribute to the Andréa Rizzo Foundation so that children with cancer could experience the emotional and physical benefits of dance therapy.

Before she knew it, Ashley was convincing her dance teacher to hold an overnight dance-a-thon at their dance studio to raise funds to support *Dréa's Dream*. With Brandon on the mend and responding well to treatment, Lynn was relieved to shift her focus from the sadness and stress and be actively involved in something that could help other children who suffered.

Within months they had organized their first dance-a-thon in New Jersey, and Ashley herself had raised $3,000 in donations from generous friends and family. As soon as I heard about this compassionate family, I notified the press about their efforts and a cover story in their local newspaper told of their compelling tale. My mom, dad, sister, brother, nieces, and nephews attended the dance-a-thon and a long-lasting friendship began between our families.

Meanwhile, in nearby Colonia, New Jersey, Dorothy Schaeffer had read of the Audets' support for the Andréa Rizzo Foundation in the newspaper with tears streaming down her face. She herself was suffering with breast cancer and her own daughter, Lauren, was an avid dancer at Purdue University. She knew that this story would touch her daughter in the same way it had moved her. She quickly snipped out the local article and sent it off to Lauren.

Dorothy was right. As soon as Lauren read the article, she wanted to make a difference, too. Cancer was an ugly villain in her life. It was killing the woman she loved most – her mother. If her own love of dance could help to ease the pain of others, she wanted to take action.

Lauren tucked the article into her dance bag and brought it to the next rehearsal of the Higher Ground Dance Company at Purdue University. All 125 dancers decided right then and there that they would donate the proceeds of their upcoming benefit performance to the Andréa Rizzo Foundation.

Inspired by the compassion of these young dancers, I wanted to be at their performance to personally express my thanks. When I arrived, the dancers flocked to me. Somehow I was able to embrace all 125, letting them know how much their support meant. But most importantly, Dorothy Schaeffer sat proudly in the audience while I stood on the stage and told the story of how these two families had connected and opened their hearts in the midst of their own pain.

Each year, both Ashley and Lauren continued to organize their fellow dancers to dance for our cause. Brandon, now in high school, continued to thrive and he too helped with the dance-a-thons, proud to have beaten his disease.

When Lauren graduated from Purdue, she returned home to help support her mom in her fight for her life. She became part of the Andréa Rizzo Foundation's annual Heart & Feet dance exhibition committee helping to plan and volunteer at the event. Lauren's mother Dorothy, her aunts Joni and Debbie along with friends, cousins, and supporters showed up in full force to support a cause that had become part of their family's fabric. When they arrived, we were waiting with open arms to let them know how much their efforts meant to us. We all rejoiced that Lauren's cousin was getting married that summer and in lieu of favors for the guests, they would make a donation to the Andréa Rizzo Foundation.

Sadly, Dorothy's cancer continued to progress and finally took her life. Upon her passing, the Schaeffer family knew that the Andréa Rizzo Foundation was a bright focus that had given Dorothy a sense of purpose during her long, debilitating disease, so in lieu of flowers, they asked that donations be made to support *Dréa's Dream* pediatric dance therapy program.

Ashley's dance school and Higher Ground Dance Company at Purdue University continued to hold benefit performances to support *Dréa's Dream* and together raised nearly $100,000 to ensure that children with cancer and special needs would receive the healing benefits of dance/movement therapy. Three families became united by their mutual battles with cancer, their love of dance, and unrelenting desire to reach past their own heartaches and help someone else. How could I not keep moving forward?

When I attended the second annual benefit held by the Higher Ground Dance Company, I entered the enormous auditorium as the dancers finished up their pre-show rehearsal. I slid into the back row and quietly sat down, hearing hushed whispers from the few dancers remaining on the stage. "That's Andréa's mother!" They were talking about me as if I were someone special. At first I was perplexed, but then realized that our story was a story they could relate to: a mother and daughter, a dancer, with a love that had transcended death.

After the performance, I stayed on to thank the dancers and felt a hand on my arm. Gina, a Purdue freshman, approached me with tears in her eyes. She poured out the story of her recent diagnosis. Cancer had spread to her leg and she was terrified that she might never dance again. She hoped dance therapy might help her once her surgery was complete.

In the now empty auditorium, we hugged, both sniffling back our tears. I promised her that we would find a way. Gina survived and became a good friend and supporter of *Dréa's Dream*.

By its sixth anniversary, *Dréa's Dream* had spread to twenty sites in both hospitals and public schools. With the help of dancers holding fundraising events coast to coast, through our Dance Across America initiative, we were providing dance therapy to thousands of children with cancer and special needs.

Fundraising didn't come easily to me. There's nothing I disliked more than asking for money. But dancers reached out to me and expressed a heartfelt interest in raising pledges or holding benefit performances, allowing the Foundation to be a channel for these young people to make a difference through their love of dance. Beautiful relationships were born among all of us based on their compassion for children in need. Who better than a dancer to understand how powerful dance could be in helping a child to heal and cope with life-threatening diseases or other special needs? Positive energy was flowing at me from all directions.

Before I knew it, I was being asked to speak about our mission. I had never spoken in front of anyone except groups of seven-year-olds. I flew to Long Beach, California, and after a harrowing flight that included a six-hour stay on the tarmac at JFK Airport in New York City, I finally stepped to the platform in the grand ballroom of the Hilton Hotel to receive an Outstanding Achievement Award bestowed upon me by the American Dance Therapy Association.

Still not comfortable with standing in front of crowds, my speech was short, and I had written every word on a small sheet of paper that quivered in my trembling hands. I was sure that I would trip on my tongue, yet words of gratitude seemed to flow out of my mouth and touch the hearts of the audience. Andréa's dream was moving through me to those who wanted to support it.

Then came another one of those serendipitous moments. I had been invited to speak at the Unity Dance Organization of America's annual meeting in New York City and as part of my presentation I gave each attendee a copy of the magazine, *Dance Studio Life*. Its feature article about the Foundation was full of photos and praise.

With magazines in place and video set to help me through the next hour, I heard laughter come from the back of the room. Rhee Gold, the publisher of *Dance Studio Life,* happened to be in the audience and was chuckling at the coincidence. I had no idea who published the magazine and obviously had never met Rhee Gold, no less expected him to be present. Not only that, but Rhee Gold was the founder of Unity Dance Organization of America. This small synchronicity led to the Rhee Gold Company's generous support in the form of a video and ultimately an honor I will never forget. I was flown to the Swan and Dolphin Resort in Orlando, Florida, to receive a Lifetime Achievement Award at the Rhee Gold Company's Dance Life Conference. This conference included 700 dancers, master dance teachers, and hundreds of vendors. I sat at the gala luncheon, hyperventilating once again, because this time I was walking onto a stage to receive an award in front of more than 700 people.

After the luncheon ended, dancers surrounded me wanting to know how they could help. Several of them shared their own stories of children with cancer or special needs. We spoke until finally the lights were dimmed, signaling that the janitors had to lock up. We exchanged emails and reluctantly said goodbye. I slowly walked back to my hotel room full of added strength and resolve. As Andréa's dream brought me love and support, my grief became a manageable monster.

September 2009

Another school year was underway and I would begin my balancing act once again. I was walking through Walmart gathering up neon colored folders and fruit-scented erasers for my new students, when my brother called me. After we greeted each other, he asked if I had been getting lots of phone calls that afternoon.

"No," I replied with a curious tone.

When he told me a friend of his had heard Jane Seymour mention me on *The View* that morning, I laughed out loud. "Why in the world would Jane Seymour be talking about ME, a second grade teacher who shops in Walmart?"

I insisted that this was absolute nonsense; there was no reason for me to be mentioned in the middle of a conversation among Barbara Walters, Joy Behar, Whoopi Goldberg, and Jane Seymour on national TV. I promised my brother I would check *The View* online when I got home. As we said our goodbyes, I chuckled to myself.

I filled my shopping basket with the basics, but even after so many years I still dodged triggers like de-frizz hair mousse and the CD aisle for fear they might send me out the door in tears. I hummed over the Muzak. The familiar songs could still add pain to a simple trip to Walmart.

At home, I unpacked all of my mundane things, putting each of them away as I grabbed a fresh bottle of water out of the fridge. I checked my phone messages, returned two calls, and then sat down with my laptop to search online for *The View*. After several tries with no success, I called my friend Barbara, knowing she would be a patient coach. I followed her directions and within minutes we found the link. Barbara stayed on the phone with me and we watched as Jane Seymour came onto the set in a flowing red dress looking absolutely stunning.

Jane was discussing her new book, *Open*

Hearts. I had bought a copy a few weeks earlier. I'd read the first half, each page of inspirational quotes, stories, and poems speaking to me and providing soothing words that became a source of peace after a long day at school.

As the interview came to a close, it became clear my brother's crazy story was just that – crazy! As I suspected, there was no mention of me. Barbara Walters said to Jane, "So this is a wonderful book full of quotes, prose, and poetry."

Jane politely stopped her and said, "Actually, it also has some very moving stories in it." She went on to speak in that lovely British accent about a mother who had begun a foundation for children with cancer and special needs.

My heart skipped a beat. But then, Barbara Walters interrupted. I held my breath. Jane quickly went on though and managed to squeeze in the rest of her description. "The woman in this story is now helping children through dance therapy."

Barbara and I were in disbelief. I ran upstairs, carrying the phone (with Barbara hanging on the other end of the line) and found my copy of *Open Hearts* on my night table. I heard Barbara telling me to hurry, but I kept repeating that this wasn't possible as I had read a good bit of this book already.

Diving onto my bed, I quickly skimmed through each page, practically ripping the edges as I hunted for a glimpse of my story. There on page 91 in beautifully inscribed lettering were the words that popped off the page and made my brother's phone call suddenly not seem crazy at all. There was my story! That book had been sitting in my own bedroom, on my night table, next to my head for weeks, and I didn't have a clue that it held a piece of my life in its pages.

October 2009

On one of those typically glorious early autumn days, the sun shone as I left school after a long day of teaching. I hoped my commute from Connecticut to Rhode Island would be traffic-free and leave me enough time for a quick walk on the beach. I grabbed my phone from my overloaded tote bag and proceeded out the door of Memorial School to my car. Typical messages awaited me – a dentist's office calling to confirm an appointment, a young dancer asking how to support the Andréa Rizzo Foundation, and then the message that made my heart stop. Jane Seymour had left me a message describing a new website for her *Open Hearts* concept. She wanted ME to come to Los Angeles to tell my story so that it could be filmed and shared on a new website. She left her home phone number and asked if I would please return her call. With my heart now racing, I sat there in the parking lot and I dialed her number. Jane Seymour answered after the second ring. She'd been waiting for my call. As I heard her explain that the filming would have to take place on October 5th, a weekday, I felt a sinking feeling. How could I leave my seven-year-old students so early in the school year? I began explaining this to Jane when I realized that I was about to turn down a chance of a lifetime. Only another doting elementary school teacher could have understood my reluctance.

I hesitated and then said, "I'll be there." Within

24 hours, I had made plane reservations and received instructions. I would have two minutes to say my piece, and I would have to say it all at once because the camera was going to be on me the whole time. There would be no cutaway shots.

Rushing out of school on a crisp October day, I headed toward the airport, rehearsing my two-minute story over and over again. I continued my incessant practicing on the six-hour flight. It was quite simple, but I was told that it had to be done in one take. How I wished they could use the wonders of editing on an amateur like me.

Touching down at midnight Pacific time, I walked off the plane to see a throng of chauffeurs awaiting passengers. One of them held a sign bearing my name in bold letters. He whisked me off to the Loews Hotel on Santa Monica Beach where a luxury room had been reserved for me. When I checked in, the concierge handed me my briefing booklet. The cover read: "Jane Seymour's *Open Hearts*." Inside was a checklist of all the particulars – even the script I had written and sent via email. Laughing out loud, I shared with him that I had just arrived straight from my second grade classroom on the east coast and this all seemed so unreal to me. With kindness in his voice, he wished me luck and assured me that I'd do a great job. He could see I needed reassuring.

Entering my room, I took a deep breath and stepped out on the curved balcony overlooking the spectacular pool and the ocean with the Santa Monica Pier lit up in the background. Filled with excitement and not worrying about the ungodly hour, I whisked out my camera. I wanted to capture everything about this luxurious setting. How else would my friends and family ever believe that I had stayed here?

I slid into the king-sized bed and prayed that I'd sleep until noon since my video shoot wasn't until 4:00 p.m. Instead, I couldn't sleep a wink and ended up beginning the day early, giving me plenty of time to get organized and prepared. Having thrown three possible outfits into my suitcase – all of them in neutral tones – I still wasn't sure what to wear. I'd been told the shoot would take place at a home in Venice Beach and the walls would be red. Not wanting to clash with the surroundings, I decided that I'd let the camera people make this decision for me and packed up my mix of sweaters and pants. What did I know about video shoots?

At 2:00 p.m., the front desk called to announce that my chauffeur awaited me in the lobby. Off I went to Venice Beach in a limo, navigating the narrow streets filled with funky colored homes. Some were large and modern, squeezed onto postage stamp sized lots – others looked more like enchanted shacks with peace signs decorating their facades. We arrived at a beach cottage that had been rented for the shoot – small but with lots of charm and character. Surrounded by palm trees and flowering bushes, a wooden fence hid the front door from view. As we entered a tall gate, I felt nervousness take hold of my stomach and make its way up my throat. I walked into the foyer and there was Jane Seymour sitting in the adjacent living room about to start the taping of her segment. Wearing a gorgeous red satin blouse, looking radiant, and as calm as could be, she paused to make me feel welcome. I instantly got butterflies when I saw the size of the crew. A roomful of cameramen!

I quietly tiptoed past them and followed an assistant upstairs – careful not to disturb Jane's segment. The hair and makeup team awaited and took over to perform their magic. The makeup artist worked on my face like it was a canvas – using enough makeup to cover a large mural. The wardrobe crew picked out a pale blue sweater from my assortment, exclaiming that it blended beautifully with the surroundings. They were all so gracious – trying to boost my confidence and calm my nerves.

An hour later, Jane Seymour came upstairs to prepare for her next segment and there I sat with rollers in my hair, in the bathroom, chatting with her while we were transformed by the same two experts. Of course, she needed very little transforming. When I let her know how nervous I felt about doing my piece in one continuous shot, she tried to reassure me. "Don't worry, you'll do fine. Just speak from your heart." At that point my heart was in my throat!

Cameras in place, I entered the room filled with ten people who were setting up for my shoot. Nerves took over as it became clear that they would all be watching ME!

Sheepishly, I asked to see my notes – just in case I blanked out.

"Notes?" the soundman asked.

"Well, yes! My mind has gone blank!"

Joking to get me to relax, they seated me in a chair within inches of the camera. This didn't help.

After a few more touch-ups on my hair and makeup, we were ready to go.

Just like in the movies, the director said, "Take one!" I plunged into my two-minute speech.

"You didn't say the words *Open Heart*!" he calmly said when I had finished.

"Can you edit it and I'll talk about my open heart now?" I asked. "I do know exactly what I am going to say about it – I just forgot."

"No. Sorry. We don't want to edit. We'd like this to look natural. Can you say all that you said all over again? Don't worry. We can do this several times. We just want the camera to be on you the whole time without interruption."

"I can't remember what I said a second ago – no less a whole spiel," I mumbled to myself, embarrassed by my inability to think straight.

We tried it again. By this time, beads of perspiration were forming and the makeup man swooped in with a brush to take away any sweaty sheen from my makeup-laden face."

Okay – Take two! Perfect! Oh, but you made a funny little grimace at the end before I said CUT."

"CUT? I didn't know you were going to say that," I responded in a meek voice.

I apologized and thankfully, he said, "It's okay – I think we can fade out before you made the funny little grimace."

Before I was able to take a sigh of relief, he

said, "Now I have a few questions for you."

"Questions?" I wasn't prepared for questions but I forged ahead. He asked what the *Open Heart* concept meant to me and I hoped my words were making sense.

"CUT! PERFECT!!"

The sound man groaned, "Oops, sorry. There was a plane going overhead and I picked it up in the system. Can we try that again?"

"Sure!" But at that point I didn't remember a thing that had come out of my very dry mouth. Repeating a slightly different version, I prayed that I had gotten in all of the basics.

As we finished up, I thanked them for their kindness – especially Jane – and gave each of them an Andréa Rizzo Foundation button tied with a yellow ribbon. My chauffeur awaited me at the door and the limo whisked me back to the hotel where I collapsed onto the bed, watching the sunset over the Pacific Ocean.

Gratitude filled that place in my heart where all of the goodness coming my way had set up residence. I could only imagine the impact that this video would have on spreading the word of *Dréa's Dream* and hoped I had done enough to help the *Open Hearts* concept. Too elated to be exhausted, I took yet another red-eye flight back to Connecticut and prayed I'd be home in time for the start of another school day. Miraculously, I was.

Don't Make Them Feel Different –

I am the one pulled out of your classroom,
I am the one who is lost,
I am the one who cries,
I am the one who is struggling,
I am the one you ignore,
I am the one who needs your help.
I am the one with learning disabilities....
Will you help me?

Andréa Rizzo
Looking Back 1997

Dréa's Dream

in Action

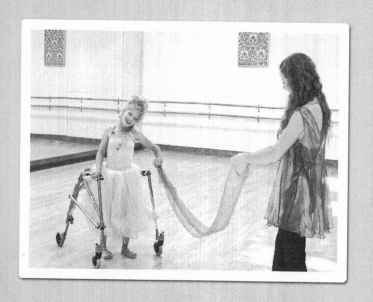

Epilogue

Winter 2011

Each February, I looked forward to a vacation with my brother, sister, and their families. We'd enjoy a week together in the Bahamas, giving us time to catch up and solidify those family bonds that brought me comfort. The upcoming year would be no different – I thought – until I looked at the calendar and saw that for the first time in my long teaching career, my school system had chosen to change our vacation to the week before President's Day rather than the week after. How could my school superintendent just up and decide to make a change like this after decades?

Then came the call that lifted me right out of my doldrums and added a huge dose of affirmation to my new life. Standing in the center of my little kitchen on an early November day, I picked up the phone expecting it to be a friend confirming our plans for a Saturday afternoon lunch.

"Hello, Susan. This is Jane Seymour."

I held the phone in silence as my heart began pumping. With that now familiar British accent, she explained that she had taken her *Open Hearts* jewelry concept one big step forward. An Inaugural Gala was planned for her newly formed Open Hearts Foundation, a nonprofit established to bring the *Open Hearts* philosophy of selfless giving despite adversity into communities worldwide. Her next words left me speechless.

I asked her to repeat what I thought she had said.

"You have been chosen as one of the first four recipients of the Open Hearts Foundation Award." My head spun, and I wondered if there had been some mistake because surely I didn't fit in with the rest of the honorees – Dallas Cowboys legend Emmitt Smith and his wife Pat, *Good Morning America* anchor Robin Roberts, President of Life Rolls On (an affiliate of the Dana and Christopher Reeve Foundation) Jesse Billauer... and me? I found it hard to speak. Instead, tears rolled down my face. Just as quickly, gratitude flooded in, and I wanted to jump right through the phone and hug her.

My excitement ignited something familiar, something I hadn't felt in too many years to count. In my old life, I might have described this as joy. At that very moment my pain was transformed into joy.

I anxiously asked Jane when the gala would take place.

"February 19th. Can you make it?"

That date fell right in the middle of the new schedule for my February vacation. (I silently praised my school superintendent for her obvious good choice in timing.)

As we continued speaking, I tried to restrain myself from jumping up and down on the kitchen tiles like a teenager having just been asked to the prom by the captain of the football team. I didn't want to hang up the phone for fear that this would somehow evaporate.

Jane explained that her new foundation would recognize those who had turned their own challenges into a triumph by simply opening their hearts to help those in need and would provide funds to charitable organizations in the areas of health, arts, education, and sports. "Your work with the Andréa Rizzo Foundation and the gift of *Dréa's Dream* pediatric dance therapy for children with cancer and special needs is the epitome of the *Open Hearts* philosophy." Jane went on to say that living with an open heart allowed for the ability to overcome adversity and create something positive. She explained that her own mother had inspired this philosophy in her and her sisters. The conversation ended with my expressing thanks, although I truly couldn't find enough words.

Then I did what every woman does when she gets exciting news. I called my friends and family and let them know every last thrilling detail. We all agreed that the coincidence of the date landing in the midst of my newly scheduled February vacation was part of the magic.

I made a little sign upward and thanked God for bringing this miracle of joy into my life. I couldn't have Andréa back with me, but her dream would be brought to the forefront because someone – Jane Seymour – cared enough to make it a reality.

When the formal invitation arrived, my hands trembled as I read the words:

*You Are Invited to the Inaugural Celebration of the
Open Hearts Foundation
Saturday, February 19, 2011
Hosted at the Private Residence
Of Jane Seymour and James Keach
Malibu, California
6:00 pm
Cocktails at Twilight
8:00 pm
Dinner
9:00 pm
Special Awards and Performances*

My name was right in the middle of the list of honorees, printed on the exquisitely designed paper bearing Jane's large red *Open Heart* symbol. Breathless, astonished, and overwhelmed – a flood of emotions welled up inside me!

When February arrived, I had to make sure I would land at LAX several days ahead of schedule so a New England nor'easter couldn't swoop in and keep me snowbound at Logan Airport in Boston. If I could have worn a surgical mask to school each day to prevent my students' sniffles and coughs from infecting me, I surely would have. Nothing would stand in the way of my having a chance to feel like a queen for one night.

After months of writing and re-writing my speech, recording myself to be sure I kept my voice animated instead of flat and predictable, practicing every morning in the car while driving to school, and even daring to beg my most non-judgmental friends to listen once I felt confident enough, I was ready for the big night in Malibu.

As I told Jane later, there would never be a wedding for me to attend as mother of the bride, so this was my once-in-a-lifetime moment – a moment that would bring the long-lost upbeat spark back into my heart and nourish my soul. I felt joy returning for the first time in almost nine years. The excitement of getting ready for that night gave me my spirit back.

After a whirlwind week in Santa Monica that included a surprise lunch at the Getty Villa with Jane and her warm and wonderful sisters visiting from England, as well as her art director, Susan, who had planned this special treat and taken care to check in on me daily, the day arrived when I would have my chance to stand at the podium before 350 people, many of them celebrities, and tell my story.

My hair, nails, and makeup appointments had cost me half a month's salary, but who cared? This was a night to splurge on. My dress, shoes, and black flouncy organza wrap (perfect for hiding my imperfect arms) were hanging outside of the bathroom in my own private bungalow – not an ordinary room by any standards – at the Fairmont Miramar.

The word bungalow conjures up something quaint like a cottage. Not this bungalow. Envision the finest draperies, spreads and linens, along with a marble and glass bathroom topped off with towels, and a bathrobe so plush I couldn't help but hug myself as I draped it around my shoulders.

Gifts awaited me on my pillow. The first one to catch my eye was a handwritten and most heartfelt note from Jane and her husband, James Keach, thanking me for coming all the way to California to help them celebrate their new charity. (Thanking *me*?) Sitting next to the card was a beautifully wrapped box that held a diamond studded *Open Heart* necklace with black accents to match my black dress. I immediately understood why Jane had asked me what color I was wearing when we sat at lunch chatting about all of the details for the upcoming evening. This thoughtful touch sent my hand straight for the Kleenex box. To top it off, there was a bottle of chardonnay from the Keach Family Vineyard, complete with Jane Seymour's own label. This was a Cinderella moment, and I couldn't imagine how I would thank them for all of their compassion and generosity. I looked up and said another silent prayer of thanks.

Following the directions left for me on my nightstand, I called the concierge (how easily we can get used to the celebrity life) to let him know that the chauffeur should pick me up at 4:00 p.m. The guests of honor were to arrive early for the red carpet photos and then the cocktails at twilight.

I had invited Dr. Lori Baudino, our California-based dance therapist, to be my guest as she had worked tirelessly to spread *Dréa's Dream* to Mattel Children's Hospital UCLA and Children's Hospital Los Angeles. She arrived early at the Fairmont Miramar so we could put any final touches on hair and makeup, and toast this night with a glass of Keach Family Vineyard wine. Having spent an hour helping each other with last-minute primping, we were like two giddy girls as we rushed through the palatial lobby and stepped into the limousine.

Breezing down the Pacific Coast Highway, I wanted to stop time. I didn't want this night to end. But I could have done without the butterflies in my stomach that were edging up into my throat. I felt anxious to get up on that stage and deliver my over-rehearsed speech. Not until that was out of the way could I thoroughly enjoy this fairytale evening.

We drove through the ornate gates, and the chauffeur phoned to the main house to announce our arrival. By now I could hardly catch my breath and wondered if I would truly be able to speak when the time came. We felt like royalty as he helped us out of the car. Melanie, my personal hostess for the evening, greeted me and ushered me to the red carpet for poses and photos. At least twelve photographers clicked away with big camera flashes, and I tried to stand the way they do at the Academy Awards, angling my position to the left and then the right. What did I know about posing on red carpets?

We approached the front door of Jane's home and stepped inside. I felt I was dreaming. Despite its beautiful gardens, pools, and ocean view, her home felt like a "real home," and that moved me the most. Photos of her children, lovingly framed, sat on the vanity in the bathroom – which by the way was our first stop because I had to check to be sure that the false eyelashes the salon planted on my eyelids had not shifted, and that my hair, lipstick, and dress were all in order. I kept reminding myself to breathe.

As we walked into the elegant foyer, we were

greeted with hugs from Jane, wearing a stunning, long, white dress. She graciously accompanied us as we floated into the spacious family room where James Keach served us some of the Keach Family Vineyard's wine and immediately made us feel welcome.

Nothing could have prepared me for what came next. Along the family room walls were large flat screens illuminated with videos that producer and director James Keach himself had created for each honoree. So there I stood, sipping wine, chatting with too many celebrities to count, and all the while I could see my face and Andréa's flashing up on the screens that surrounded us – a team again.

As the cocktail hour ended, we followed Jane into a tent the size of a stadium with at least six tall peaks pulling the billowing white cloth upward. It appeared as though we had just stepped into the land of Aladdin. Rose-colored lighting filled an ethereal space and made the night suddenly turn magical.

The next thing we knew, we were seated at the front table at the foot of the stage with Jane and the other honorees. Fragrant flowers covered every surface and the *Open Hearts* design was woven into every arrangement. I found out weeks later, when a vase full of exquisite blooms arrived at my door in Rhode Island, that Jane's silk botanical line had been mixed in with the fresh flowers that night. I will forever have them to treasure as a remembrance of that incredible evening. This last thoughtful touch still overwhelms me.

As I sat down, Melanie introduced me to the stage director. I breathed a sigh of relief when he informed me that I'd be the first of the honorees to speak, and that he'd give me a signal when that time arrived. I knew I'd have forgotten every word I wanted to say if I had to follow the other prestigious honorees.

Before I knew it, he was escorting me to the side of the stage to sit discreetly out of the way while they played my introductory video.

Hands sweaty, legs shaking, unable to breathe, and trying to hold back my tears, I watched the emotional video created by James Keach about Andréa and me as it played on four huge screens throughout the tent. With tears at the tips of my false eyelashes, I made a Herculean effort to keep my emotions in check while Jane introduced me. I was sure the chair I was perched on stage-side must have been visibly vibrating, giving away my panicked nervousness to all who sat nearby.

I couldn't allow myself to think about the audience. I would just have to be myself – a second grade teacher from New England with a deep love for her daughter and an enormous will to see her dream become a reality.

And then in a booming voice, the announcer said, "Ladies and Gentlemen, please welcome to the stage, Susan Rizzo Vincent."

I vividly remember standing tall and walking assertively across the stage. If I acted self-assured then I *might* sound self-assured. I met Jane's embrace and proudly received my Open Heart Foundation Award – a large, fine art, bronze sculpture, beautifully shaped into the *Open Heart* symbol, and engraved with my name on the marble base. I thought of Emmitt Smith's encouraging words: "Speak from your heart." And I did.

Looking out at the sea of faces, it all made sense. Although our lives had been sent on an unimaginable and unexpected course, Andréa and I had maintained an unbreakable bond – like a dance that never ended – reaching back decades and now extending from heaven to earth. Our story was one that not only helped the neediest of children, but also touched people's hearts.

There wasn't a dry eye anywhere as I delivered my carefully rehearsed speech. I began to breathe easier as I shared stories of children and the impact dance therapy had made on their treatment and their healing. The hush of the crowd was a silent affirmation that all of our hard work as a mother and daughter team would continue.

The words began to roll off my lips:

Let me ask you to imagine a ten-year-old pediatric cancer patient named Christopher. His childhood has been stolen from him. After his daily bouts with chemotherapy his lungs have filled with fluid. He is so weak and so frail. A dance therapist enters his hospital room and has him swinging his arms, spinning, and dancing to the music. As he shakes his little body to the rhythm, he releases his pent up energy and is beaming from ear to ear. The hospital room is transformed from a sick room into a well room. We all know how good it feels to dance! After his therapy session the doctors said his "happy dance" had helped clear his lungs and spared him a stay in the pediatric intensive care unit.

That is the work of the Andréa Rizzo Foundation.

Today, Dréa's Dream pediatric dance therapy program, funded by the Andréa Rizzo Foundation, is helping children with cancer and special needs through "one on one" and small group sessions in twenty sites across the country. This includes schools, Ronald McDonald Houses and some of our nation's most renowned hospitals, such as Children's Hospital Los Angeles, Mattel Children's Hospital UCLA, and Memorial Sloan-Kettering Cancer Center. All of this has been accomplished completely through volunteer effort.

I couldn't believe this was me – standing up with such calm and confidence. I continued:

In each and every site, a licensed dance therapist funded by the Foundation provides a clinical model for children with cancer and special needs to overcome their fear, frustration, anger, and anxiety as well as their physical challenges. Whether it's a child with cancer or a child with autism, the dance therapist is trained to access those emotions through dance and movement. Dance therapy has become a highly regarded healing modality in integrative medicine.

I was coming toward the end and prayed that I'd make it through without faltering as the words kept flowing.

I have been an elementary school teacher my whole life. In June, I will leave the classroom to focus all of my energy on making the benefits of Dréa's Dream available to more hospitals and more fragile children – children like Christopher with his "happy dance."

I can now say, beyond a shadow of doubt, that through this incredible journey, my heart is fully open and Andréa's dream lives on through each child, each doctor, each dance therapist, each volunteer who never quits – and now all of you who have been so kind to listen to my story this evening. When we live with an open heart we use our lives to illuminate something larger.

I extended my sincerest thanks to Jane, James Keach, and the Open Hearts Foundation and, as I sat back down, Emmitt Smith smiled his one-of-a-kind smile and spoke to me like a proud coach. "You did it!"

Lori and I hugged and burst into tears. All of the raw emotion that had built up over weeks and months came pouring out. The tears shed at this momentous event made an inexplicable difference for me in my healing. I could actually feel my spirit begin to soar – the upbeat spirit that I thought had been forever lost.

With all of the sensitivity that comes from being the mother of six, Jane Seymour had recognized my story as an expression of hope for children and had given me an incredible opportunity to share it with many influential people. In addition, all the honorees received an overwhelmingly generous donation to perpetuate the work of their charitable organizations. Dance as therapy would now impact so many more fragile young lives in the same way that it had helped Andréa overcome all of her challenges. I thought of every child, every dancer, and Andréa.

As the fairy tale evening came to an end, I

stood and turned to find a long line of people waiting to shake my hand and tell me how moved they were by our story. I knew Andréa's dream would spread far and wide.

The next day came too soon. I would have to trade in my glass slippers for snow boots as the limousine headed toward the airport and the radio newscaster announced an impending storm in the Northeast. I didn't want to leave behind all of the wonder of this life-altering week. I wanted to make it last forever. I glowed inside, and it felt so good.

I reluctantly entered the American Airlines entrance at LAX. As I went through security, I had a good laugh as the security guards pulled my large, stunning, bronze Open Hearts Foundation Award from my carry-on along with an empty bottle of Keach Family Vineyard wine. I blurted out my story to them as quickly as I could.

Unexpectedly, one of the guards remarked, "Ma'am, I hear lots of stories coming through this line, and yours just about made me cry."

It felt strange to see a brawny man in a TSA uniform turn away from the X-ray images and really look me in the eye. He seemed to connect with the pain and joy of my hastily babbled tale. "Oh, thank you, that's so kind. I'd rather have my daughter here with me, but at least I can make a difference through her Foundation." I still found it hard to speak about the positives that were creeping back into my life without acknowledging my heartache.

"I think anyone would feel the same." He

nodded, pushing my luggage further down the line. "You should write a book."

A book... "I might just do that."

I thought of our book as I dragged my luggage down the long corridor, headed for Gate 22. I knew with certainty that the time had come for the written account I'd been crafting together to become more than just a holiday project for me. It was time to stop fiddling and finish the work Andréa and I had promised to collaborate on so many years ago.

Our book could bring hope to parents of children with cancer. Our book would offer possibilities and inspiration to children with learning disabilities.

Our book would transform lives with its message of hope, love, and the power of dance, just as the Foundation did – just as my beautiful Andréa had always done.

During the flight home, I settled in and relaxed my head on the headrest while looking out the window at the clouds – always feeling a little closer to heaven when airborne. I pondered all that had transpired over these last nine years. There were so many children to live and dance for. Together, Andréa and I would dance on.

Miracle of Life

My mother always tells me what a miracle it is that I am alive and healthy. She never imagined I would go on to be a successful dancer and athlete after all I had been through medically. To this day my medical history has been with me and has helped to strengthen me to progress to the person I am today. I owe so much to the intern who found my tumor, neuroblastoma, and the reason for the loss of all of my motor coordination. With this surgery, if it is not found before age two, your life could end within a few short years. There were prayer groups praying for me while I was in the hospital and I know this helped pull me through surgery. I am so thankful to God, my doctors, nurses, and family for caring so much and doing everything possible to ensure my good health. I am grateful to be alive today and appreciate life so much.

Andréa Rizzo

May 1991

Grandparents, Aunts, Uncles and Cousins at walk-a-thon.

Jane Seymour's donated Open Heart Painting and Susan receives Open Hearts Foundation award.

"Life may not be the party

we hoped for,

but while we are here

we should dance."

~author unknown

Further
Acknowledgments

Special thanks to:

The Children of Misty's Dance Unlimited, LLC, Onalaska, WI, who permitted me to grace these pages with their beautiful photos.

The Narragansett Library, St. Andrew's Lutheran Church, Dave's Coffee and Galapagos Collection in Charlestown, RI for the use of their "quiet rooms."

Dedicated and supportive friends, family, and Board Members of The Andréa Rizzo Foundation who never forget the dream:

Jessica Abatemarco • Joan & Patrick Alix • Daniel Amaral • Audet Family • George Bassil • Erin & Mike Bates • Michael Battaglia • Melissa & Eric Bergman • Paige & Kenny Boudreau • Kalene Brennan • Christine& Bill Brosnan • Michael Buchwald • Amanda Burman • Jennifer & Christopher Caiozzo • Rich & Lisa Caraviello • Brianna Carter • Ryan Casupanon • Kathy Cieplik • Jennifer Cho • Close Family • Fred Colen • Maire & Frank Conisella • Michele & Mike Coppa • Denise Cronen • Madison & Meghan Cullinan • Helen & Dave Curylo • Morgan & Matthew Daly • John & Meg DeCubellis • Janice De Frances• Claudette & Michael Downey • Katie Dugan & Tony Moore • Dugan Family • Sheila Enos • Eid Family • Kaitlin Falk • Kathy & Andy Falke • Fern Family • Gina & Lee Favata • Patti Finch • Jackie Fiora • Ana Gallegos • Michaela & Bill Gardner • Billie & Gerry Gerkey • Germain Family • Rhee Gold • Chris Gray • Kerri Green • Emily & WB Hames • Jessica Hassell • Nancy & Jim Heagney • Joseph & Margaret Hegmann • Jackie Henderson • Lee Ann Hooper • Neil Jackson • Eileen & Capers Jones • Harold Joyce • Carol & Rich Kelly • Mckenzie Kelly • Patty Majeski Kerekes •

Melissa & James Keyte • Mike Kirtley • Carolyn & Ray Larrivee • Austin Lema • Faith & Manny MacDonald • Max Matt • Rich & Gail Mauch • Mike Magers • Elena McCord • Sandy Mehlman • Arthur Mercante Jr. • Jenn Moitoso • Michelle Montanano • Sharon & Cole Mulcahy • Amanda Narciso • Andrew Nguyen • Mary & Lou Orgera • Cara Passarelli • Kerri Peterson • Greg & Carol Jean Plunkett • Barbara Pomfret • Jean & Ed Pontbriant • Sarah Puerini • Vicki & Jesse Pugh • Josh Quagliarol • Rabuse Family • Julie Reed • Stacey Reed • Renshaw Family • Kimberly Rice • Norma & Richard Rosenberg • Jo-Anne Rubin • Amanda Russ • Garrett Russ • Lauren Schaeffer • Terry & Steve Schimmel • John Secor • Gabrielle Shultis • Bill Silkes • Rosemary Slocum • Lanie Smith • Susan Sonner • Kaylee Spillane • Tracie Stanfield • Jennifer St. Peter • Bill Silkes • Birdie Tarulli • Vin Testa • Chandler Tittle • Mary Jane Traska • Elena Vazintaris • Robert & Marguerite Verone • Deana & Robert Verone • Robynne Vieira • Claire Wasserman • Sarah Wasserman • Chris & John Webb • Maureen West • Jennifer Whitley • Joel Yapching • Young Family • Laura Yuen • Michele & Benny Zalewski • Ginny Zitzkat • Aurora Zapatos

Every staff member at Memorial School, East Hampton, Connecticut; Narragansett Elementary School and Ashaway Elementary School in Rhode Island who keep Andréa's memory alive through gardens and book projects.

The staff and students of Salve Regina University for their ongoing support of Dréa's Dream, especially the SRU Dance Team.

The staff at Memorial Sloan-Kettering Cancer Center for giving Andréa the gift of life and nurturing her dream into a reality.

The Andréa Rizzo Foundation's National Spokesperson, Carrie Ann Inaba.

Open Hearts Foundation for their encouragement and belief in the Andréa Rizzo Foundation's mission:
www.OpenHeartsFoundation.org
www.JaneSeymour.com
For Jane Seymour's fine art:
www.CoralCanyonPublishing.com

Dance Therapists who bring the gift of Drea's Dream to children with cancer and special needs:

Jean Basiner, MA, R-DMT- RI & FL
Lori Baudino, Psy.D., BC-DMT- CA
Becky Brittain, Ph.D., R-DMT- MO
Heidi Fledderjohn, MA-BC-DMT- IN
ToniFreni, MS, BC-DMT- NJ
Rosanna Hernandez, MS, R-DMT- NY
Sharon Mulcahy, MA, R- DMT- CT
Melissa Sabatini, MA, R- DMT- RI
Jocelyn Shaw, MA, BC-DMT- NY
Suzi Tortora, Ed.D., BC-DMT- NY
Lisa Troisi, MA, R- D MT - CO
Jennifer Whitley, MS, R-DMT- NY

All of the staff at the schools and hospitals where Drea's Dream lives on:

Alvin Ailey Arts in Education, NY
Cardinal Glennon Children's Hospital, MO
Children's Hospital Los Angeles, CA
Connecticut Children's Medical Center, CT
Hasbro Children's Hospital, RI
Herbert Richardson 21st Century School, NJ
Ignazio Cruz Early Childhood Center, NJ
J.M Rapport School, NYC
John Street School, NY
Mass General Hospital, MA
Mattel Children's Hospital UCLA, CA
Memorial Elementary School, CT
Memorial Hospital, CO
Memorial Sloan-Kettering Cancer Center, NY
Narragansett Elementary School, RI
Riley Hospital for Children, IN
Ronald McDonald House, NY
St. Joseph's Children's Hospital, FL
West Warwick High School, RI

Thanking every dancer, dance school and dance company who has supported Drea's Dream through our Dance Across America fundraising initiative:

All That Dance, Jackson, NJ
Arts in Motion, Matawan, NJ
Art in Motion, No. Kingstown, RI
Arthur Murray Dance Studios, Glastonbury & Bloomfield, CT
ARTSYOUniversity, Hamilton, NJ
Astoria Dance Centre, Astoria, NY
Ballet Arts Centre, Winchester, MA
Band of Gypsies, NYC
Binghamton University Ballroom Dancers, NY
Border Crossing Collective, NYC
Broadway Dance Center, Arts in Motion Youth, NYC
Briarcliff HS Dance Program, Briarcliff Manor, NY
Cambridge Street Dance Academy, Mt. Pleasant, SC
Center Stage Dance Studio, Stamford, CT
Champagne Girls, Non-Profit Entertainers, Branchville, NJ
City Dance, Perth Amboy, NJ
Competitors' Closet, Warwick, RI
Connecticut Dance School, Fairfield, CT
Corliss Whitney's Seasoned Steppers of Ms. NY Sr. America
Creativity in Motion, Coatesville, PA
Dance Expressions Competition, No. Wales, PA
Dance On Hudson, Croton on Hudson, NY
Dance Concepts, Farmingdale, NJ
Dance Factor, Fords, NJ
Dancers Against Cancer, UCLA, Los Angeles, CA
Dancing Wheels, Cleveland, OH
Danceworks, Hofstra University, NY
Defying Gravity School of Dance, Warwick, RI
Edison School of Music & Dance, Edison, NJ
Fusion Dance Centre, Kenilworth, NJ
Gladdings School of Dance, Newport, RI
Gulliver Preparatory, Coral Gables, FL
Higher Ground Dance Co., Purdue University, IN
Huntington High School, Huntington, WV
ICON Dance Complex Dancers, NYC
Just Dance! Dance Company, Framingham, MA

Kinetic Synergy Dance Company, Weymouth, MA
KMC Dance, Kennett Square, PA
Lawrence High School, Cedarhurst, NY
Linton Dance, Dobbs Ferry, NY
M & T Dance Studio, Seaford, NY
Michelle Ciotta & Kristin Brazalovich Zumbathon, CT
Misty's Dance Unlimited, LLC, WI
Naganuma Dance Co., NYC
Nelia Lawton's Providence Ballroom and Jazz Project, RI
Nevins Academy of Irish Dancers, Newport, RI
Next Stage Project, NYC
New England American Dance Therapy Assoc., MA
North Kingstown High School, RI
Not Just Dance LLC, Clermont, FL
Oxford High School, Oxford, CT
Pikes Peak Performance Company, CO
Positions Dance Studio, Babylon, NY
Providence Academy of International Studies, RI
Rhythm & Moves School of Music and Dance, Edison, NJ
Riverside Dance Center, Riverside, RI
Rosemary School of Dance Education, Warren, RI
Saito Dance Co., University of Michigan, Ann Arbor, MI
South Jersey Performing Arts Group, Stratford, NJ
SRU DANCE Salve Regina University, Newport RI
Steps Alive, Franklin Square, NY
St. Louis Academy of Dance, Pazzaz Performers, MO
Tiger Dance Co., Bluffton High School, IN
Tori Breedlove's Dance- a- thon, Macomb, IL
Tracie Stanfield's Synthesis Dance Project, NYC
Triumph Charter Academy, Los Angeles, CA
Walter Johnson High School, Bethesda, MD
Washington State HS Dance Teams Dance-a-thon, WA
Wilton Dance Studio, Wilton, CT
Vissi Dance Theater, NYC
Wilton Dance Studio, Wilton, CT

A portion of the proceeds of the sale of this book will support The Andréa Rizzo Foundation.

You can purchase *Dréa's Dream*: An Unfinished Dance online at:

www.SusanRizzoVincent.com
www.amazon.com

For more information on The Andréa Rizzo Foundation and *Dréa's Dream* pediatric dance therapy programming visit:

www.DreasDream.org

To make a tax deductible donation to
The Andréa Rizzo Foundation go to:

www.DreasDream.org

Checks may be made payable to:
The Andréa Rizzo Foundation
10 East Beach Road
Charlestown, RI 02813

If you would like Susan Rizzo Vincent to speak at your event or do a book signing, contact:

SRizzoVincent@gmail.com or phone: 401.952.2423

www.SusanRizzoVincent.com

Made in the USA
Charleston, SC
10 March 2013